THE NATIONAL STUDY OF
MILLIONAIRES

Findings From the Research Study Behind Chris Hogan's *Everyday Millionaires*

RAMSEY
PRESS

Published by Ramsey Press, The Lampo Group, LLC
Franklin, Tennessee 37064

This publication is designed to provide accurate and authoritative information with regard to the subject matter covered. It is sold with the understanding that the publisher is not engaged in rendering financial, accounting, or other professional advice. If financial advice or other expert assistance is required, the services of a competent professional should be sought.

Research: Tony Lemonis, Jameson Murray, Tim Smith, and Natalie Wilson
Editorial: Bob Bunn, Rachel Knapp, Jonathan Sims, and Cathy Shanks
Product Management: Gretchen Fagan and Amy McCollom
Design: Chris Carrico, Alex Scott, Gretchen Hyer, and Mandi Cofer

ISBN: 978-1-942121-27-5

Printed in the United States of America
20 21 22 23 24 POL 5 4 3 2 1

TABLE OF CONTENTS

INTRODUCTION

In the summer of 2017, factors within and outside of Ramsey Solutions led to ongoing conversations about what is required for individuals to experience financial independence in contemporary America. Those factors eventually led to the research that became the supporting framework for Chris Hogan's #1 national best-selling book, *Everyday Millionaires*.

Inside Ramsey Solutions, Chris Hogan and the Ramsey Solutions research team began discussing the best way to define financial independence. For several years, this conversation had centered around the idea of "retirement." The publication of Hogan's first book, *Retire Inspired*, proved to be a commercial success and provided a common language for encouraging individuals to build wealth and plan for financial security in the future within that context.

However, questions were raised about whether or not that was the *best* way to think about building wealth and creating financial independence. Eventually, the term "millionaire" ("net-worth millionaire," in particular) started gaining momentum. The idea of becoming a millionaire seemed to resonate better with the target audience and provided a clear milestone for individuals to track their progress toward financial independence. It also suggested that a person could become financially secure even before reaching the point of retirement.

Meanwhile, outside of Ramsey Solutions, another important narrative had begun taking shape in the larger culture. According to this narrative, reaching millionaire status was becoming much more difficult. Many believed that economic stagnation and limited opportunities were making it harder for average people to get ahead—much less acquire $1 million in net worth.

Some 25 years ago, Dr. Thomas Stanley conducted a study that set the standard in the area of millionaire research. The results of his pioneering work were published in his influential book, *The Millionaire Next Door*. For years to come, Stanley's influential research served as a road map toward financial independence. However, some—perhaps many—in the culture were starting to express doubts that the clear path Stanley had identified through his groundbreaking research was still viable in a contemporary context.

The convergence of these two lines of thinking convinced Chris Hogan and the research team to initiate a statistically significant project to determine how millionaires gained their wealth and what factors were necessary for the average person in America to reach net-worth millionaire status themselves. This study was called the National Study of Millionaires, and it became the largest research project of its kind ever conducted.

The working hypothesis for the study was that millionaires gain wealth through specific choices, such as working hard, demonstrating financial discipline, and investing consistently and wisely over time. These behaviors had served as core teaching points for Ramsey Solutions for more than two decades. Therefore, in addition to identifying what was happening in the culture, the study also helped determine if these were still valid talking points for the organization moving forward.

While Hogan and the other members of the research team were not sure that this working hypothesis would be affirmed, anecdotal evidence through interaction with the Ramsey Solutions audience pointed in that direction. In contrast, the null hypothesis for the study was based on perceived assumptions in society: Millionaires build wealth through advantages not available to most people. Such factors included large inheritances, luck, family backgrounds, prestigious educational backgrounds and large salaries.

RESEARCH METHODOLOGY

RESEARCH OVERVIEW

The research for the National Study of Millionaires included four phases. In the first phase, more than 50 random millionaires were interviewed to collect qualitative data. This information was used to shape the survey that collected quantitative data for the next phase of the research.

In the second phase, Chris Hogan worked with the other members of the research team to examine the results of the interviews and to develop the quantitative survey. This survey tool was distributed to 2,000 randomly sampled millionaires. The data gathered from these individuals represented the primary research for the study and were used to determine the validity of the working hypothesis. It should be noted that these millionaires were drawn from "white space"—individuals not affiliated with Ramsey Solutions—to help ensure that convenience bias was not an issue.

The third phase of the project focused on millionaires who were part of the Ramsey Solutions "tribe." Eight thousand net-worth millionaires who were members of various Ramsey Solutions email lists, along with individuals who responded to requests made during *The Dave Ramsey Show* radio programs, were included in this phase.

Since this was a convenience sample drawn from the Ramsey audience, the main purpose of this phase was to compare and contrast their responses with data collected from the white space. While a great deal of similarity existed between the two groups, the 2,000 randomly sampled white space responses were given greater emphasis in the book and in validating the working hypothesis when the data diverged.

The final phase of the study involved a random sample of 2,000 people from the general population. This provided a way to compare the characteristics of net-worth millionaires with the habits and lifestyles of those who are not millionaires. Being able to compare millionaires with the general population also allowed Hogan and the research team to address the question of survivorship bias.

In some cases, the research team was able to collect general population data from larger, recognized sources, such as the U.S. Census Bureau, the Bureau of Labor Statistics and other government data sources. When this demographic information or general data was available, the team relied on that information. When such information could not be located in a broad, general database, the team used the random sample from the general population study.

QUALITATIVE INTERVIEWS

As noted, the initial phase of the National Study of Millionaires involved a qualitative study of millionaires. The interviews in this phase allowed Hogan and the other researchers to determine key topics and insights that could be used to create a valid quantitative survey instrument for the primary focus of the study.

It should be emphasized that the research team recognized the importance of random sampling and made that a priority from the earliest stages of the project. Toward that end, the team began by vetting a number of outside panel providers who could recruit, profile and activate studies for both the specific population of millionaires and for the general population. As part of the vetting process, the research team narrowed the list of potential providers down to three and, eventually, to one nationally recognized and respected group.

The panel providers were given initial instructions to identify a sample of at least 50 millionaires from across the country for the qualitative portion of the study. They also were given parameters about how "millionaire" should be defined for the purposes of this research, since the term can mean different things to different people. For example, some define millionaires as those earning $1 million a year while others define them as having "liquid" assets equaling $1 million on hand.

Hogan and the research team chose to include only net-worth millionaires. This definition includes anyone whose assets minus liabilities equal at least $1 million. Financial independence served as a key driver for the research, and the team believed that "net worth" provides the best indicator for such independence.

The panel providers identified 53 randomly selected millionaires for the qualitative interviews. These individuals were compensated for their participation, receiving $100 in exchange for their responses. The interviews were conducted by telephone between August 11, 2017, and September 8, 2017. At least two researchers were present for each conversation. One researcher served as a moderator, while a second researcher noted responses. The interviews were also recorded for later content analysis.

Each interview lasted at least 60 minutes and provided both autobiographical and sociological data points. The millionaires were encouraged to share details of their early lives, as well as information on their career history. This gave researchers an opportunity to understand the millionaires' personal backgrounds and the role employment played in reaching net-worth millionaire status. Researchers also asked the participants about their financial habits and what they believed to be the key factors in becoming a millionaire. This part of the interview focused on things that helped them reach their goals, along with obstacles they had to overcome.

Researchers also encouraged the millionaires to share their thoughts on topics such as philanthropy and retirement, habits and routines, and hobbies and interests. After each interview was completed, its audio file and digital notes were saved. A researcher wrote a brief synopsis of the interview, and key terms were tagged as part of the process. Once all the interviews had been completed, common themes were identified and used to guide the next phase of the project: survey development for the quantitative stages.

QUANTITATIVE DESIGN AND SAMPLING

Maintaining the integrity of the National Study of Millionaires was a primary concern for Chris Hogan and the other members of the research team throughout the process. For example, the use of qualitative interviews to guide survey development for later quantitative research represents a best practice in statistically significant research. Such interviews allow researchers to identify common themes and pain points within the target audience, which strengthens the viability of the quantitative research instrument.

Content analysis of the qualitative interviews provided direction for the development of the survey questions. The research team spent two weeks in September 2017 writing possible questions and grouping them based on topic and general flow. Throughout the rest of the month, the survey questions underwent a series of stages and gates through which Hogan and the team refined them and moved them toward final approval. The early days of October 2017 were dedicated to questionnaire testing and refinement. A selection of millionaires from the Ramsey Solutions audience were used to validate the questionnaire and provide additional feedback.

Once the questionnaire was finalized, the panel providers identified 1,000 randomly selected millionaires from outside the Ramsey Solutions audience for distribution. This list included individuals from across the nation and fit the definition of net-worth millionaires.

While it was agreed that this sample would provide statistical significance and maintain the study's integrity by keeping the results within a +/- 3% margin of error, Ramsey Solutions also desired the largest research population possible. With that in mind, an additional 1,000 millionaires were added to the random sample.

To further strengthen the sampling process, the panel providers used an invitation-only, double opt-in process. Once potential study participants were identified and vetted, they were extended an invitation to join the project. To join, the millionaires had to accept the invitation and complete a second opt-in feature to provide additional vetting and validation of their qualifications to participate in the study.

QUESTIONNAIRE CATEGORIES

The questionnaire used for the quantitative stages of the National Study of Millionaires included 119 questions. Of those, 115 were distributed across eight general categories. Four additional screener questions were added to strengthen the vetting process. The general categories were broken down as follows:

- Childhood Background (14 questions)
- Family/Relationships (9 questions)
- Career History (10 questions)
- Purchasing/Money Habits (22 questions)
- Achieving High Net Worth (12 questions)
- Myths About Millionaires (10 questions)
- Millionaire Characteristics (30 questions)
- Demographics (8 questions)

The eight general categories were developed through analysis of the qualitative interviews and were designed to help the research team better understand the factors that have influenced—and continue to influence—the financial lives of net-worth millionaires. Below is a brief summary of what each category sought to define.

1. **Childhood Background**: The questions in this category sought to delve into the socioeconomics of the participants' upbringings. This included their parents' work histories and their families' standards of living growing up (i.e., upper class, middle class, lower class and so forth). Researchers also sought to understand the family dynamics of the millionaires' backgrounds, such as whether they came from a divorced or intact family unit and how many siblings they had. They were also asked to describe their educational experiences, including their college choices and their college grade-point averages (GPAs), if they had attended college.

2. **Family/Relationships**: The questions in this category examined the millionaires' current family structures. In addition to their ages, the participants were asked to give special focus to their marital status. For members of the sample who were married (a large percentage of participants), researchers encouraged them to share how long they have been married and to rate their marriage (i.e., great, good, okay, in crisis). Millionaires were also asked how many children they had and, when appropriate, their children's ages.

3. **Career History**: The questions in this category focused on what millionaires do for a living. The survey asked them to share their primary occupation and how long they had been in that profession. Questions about salary history included three sub-categories: by decade (1970s–2010s), by individual earning, and by household earning. Millionaires were also asked to describe their level of passion toward their work.

4. **Purchasing/Money Habits**: The questions in this category considered the way the millionaires in the study have handled their resources in the past and how they currently manage their money. Topics included past vehicle and home purchases, as well as budgeting and spending issues. Participants were asked about their primary expenses each month and what kind of debt they have had or continue to carry.

5. **Achieving High Net Worth**: The questions in this category examined the methods participants used to attain net-worth millionaire status. In addition to listing the value of their assets and liabilities to determine estimated net worth, the millionaires were asked about their financial planning practices and what they perceived to be the major factors in their ability to reach financial independence. This included topics such as investing strategies, inheritances, savings habits, real estate assets and utilizing a professional advisor.

6. **Beliefs About Millionaires**: The questions in this category asked participants to discuss some common cultural beliefs about how millionaires build their wealth. The members of the millionaire sample were asked to rate their responses to the following perceived beliefs:

    - Millionaires inherit their wealth.
    - Millionaires use debt to build wealth.
    - Millionaires use large incomes to build wealth.
    - Millionaires experience more luck than average people.

    Participants were also asked to use a five-point Likert scale ranging from "strongly disagree" to "strongly agree" to describe their response to the following statement: "If you're born into a poor family, you can't become wealthy."

7. **Millionaire Characteristics**: The questions in this category related to the personal qualities of each millionaire in the study. Researchers asked participants to describe such things as their attitudes toward setting goals and personal disciplines. They were also asked about personal values and motivations, as well as their approach to lifelong learning.

8. **Demographics**: The questions in this category covered the typical personal information for this type of category. Topics such as gender, age and city of residence were included.

ADDITIONAL QUANTITATIVE RESEARCH

As noted above, the core of the research was based on questionnaires distributed to a random sample of 2,000 net-worth millionaires from across the country. These millionaires were enlisted by a third-party panel provider and had no prior relationship with Ramsey Solutions. They were carefully vetted prior to receiving the survey questionnaire in an effort to provide the research with the greatest degree of statistical significance possible.

In addition, Hogan and the research team were curious about how the results from the white space participants compared to the actions and attitudes of millionaires within their own "tribe." To answer this question, Hogan and the other researchers added a third phase to the project using an 8,000-member convenience sample drawn from a group that has become known as "Ramsey Millionaires." These individuals were recruited from various database lists owned by Ramsey Solutions, as well as callouts from *The Dave Ramsey Show* radio program.

Again, it should be noted that the responses from this sample, while larger than the white space sampling, were used only for comparison purposes. In general, the random sample of millionaires and the convenience sample of Ramsey Millionaires showed alignment in many areas. However, where the two groups differed, Hogan and the research team deferred to the random sample to maintain the study's integrity and statistical significance.

For example, the two groups showed discernable differences in the area of debt history. As one might expect, many millionaires who were part of the Ramsey Solutions audience began with a larger amount of debt and worked their way through Dave Ramsey's 7 Baby Steps to build wealth over time. As a result, their debt history was far different from the white space millionaires who learned to avoid debt early in life and never had to overcome that obstacle in building wealth. In that case, the researchers leaned heavily on the random sample and referred to the Ramsey Millionaires only as a point of comparison.

Finally, Hogan and the research team completed a fourth phase of the study by enlisting a random sampling of 2,000 non-millionaires. This group served as a general population sample that could be used for additional comparisons. The research team wanted to avoid survivorship bias, which occurs when data collection focuses only on a given target population (net-worth millionaires) and ignores those outside the target (non-millionaires). The random general population sample addresses this concern.

When possible, the research team also made use of generally recognized sources that typically have extensive and respected databases, such as census data and other government reports. When databases that included comparative information could not be found, the team depended on the random sampling of the general population.

SUMMARY OF RESULTS

A team of four researchers from the Ramsey Solutions research team worked to analyze the results collected from the quantitative phases of the research. From that analysis, along with coded information drawn from the qualitative interviews, Chris Hogan and the team developed several assets. Upon conclusion of that asset creation, Hogan and the other members of the research team worked with the Ramsey Solutions editorial team to develop a statistically significant narrative of millionaires in America. This collaboration took place throughout 2018.

The most obvious result of this collaboration was the publication of *Everyday Millionaires*, released in January 2019. Overall, the book refers to more than 140 individual net-worth millionaire statistics taken from the quantitative study, along with 29 stories drawn from the millionaires who participated in the qualitative interviews. It should be noted that, to protect the anonymity of those individuals, their names and locations were changed with their permission. The stories, however, were left intact.

MILLIONAIRE DEMOGRAPHIC INFORMATION

The 2,000 randomly sampled participants in the study represented a variety of age groups. They also were drawn from every region of the country. The information in the following sections reveals some key demographic data about the net-worth millionaires in the study, especially in relation to age and geography.

MILLIONAIRES' AGES

The average millionaire in this study was 63 years old. As *Figure 1* demonstrates, a vast majority of those who had attained net-worth millionaire status were at least 45 years old. Only 7% were younger than 45, while almost three-fourths of the millionaires were at least 55 (74%).

Figure 1 Age Distribution of Millionaire Study Participants

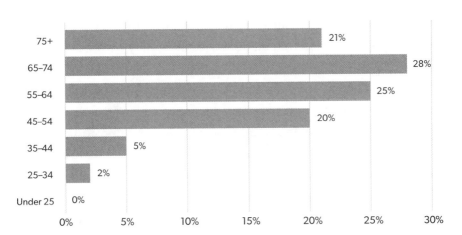

Chris Hogan and the other members of the research team expected this finding. It takes time for individuals to rise to net-worth millionaire status, so it should not be surprising that most of these individuals are older. While the sample did include some 20-something or 30-something millionaires, their numbers pale in comparison to those who have spent more time in the workforce earning and investing money.

From a generational perspective, the results were essentially the same. Only 2% of the net-worth millionaires in the study were

Millennials and 18% were from Generation X. The vast majority of participants were members of the Baby Boomer (54%) and Silent (26%) generations. While social researchers often differ on the precise definitions and ranges of these generational groups, it seems safe to state that more millionaires are members of older generations than younger generations.

But this does not mean that members of younger generations do not have the potential to become net-worth millionaires at some point. They may just need more time to earn and invest money so they can build more wealth. This research indicates that if members of younger generations are diligent over time, they can become net-worth millionaires in their own right.

In addition to age distribution, researchers asked participants to identify the ages at which they became net-worth millionaires. Again, as one might expect, the numbers skewed older. **The median age for attaining millionaire status was 50 years old**. Assuming individuals entered the workforce around 22 years old, this means that many of them took between 25–30 years to become millionaires. As noted above, this emphasizes the importance of diligence over time and helps explain why fewer millionaires identified with younger generations.

Figure 2 Age When Participants Became Millionaires

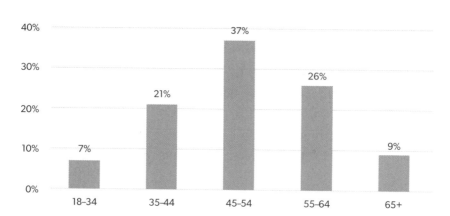

THE NATIONAL STUDY OF MILLIONAIRES

As *Figure 2* reveals, more than one-third of the millionaires in the study (37%) said they reached that status between 45–54 years old. Another 26% became millionaires between 55–64 years old. Only 7% were millionaires by the time they were 34.

Interestingly, only 9% of the respondents stated that they became millionaires after the age of 65. Stated another way, more than nine out of 10 net-worth millionaires reached financial independence before the traditional age of retirement and the start of Social Security payouts. These findings suggest that individuals should focus on making wise financial decisions during their prime earning years (approximately 35–64), because it is much more difficult—though not impossible—to reach millionaire status after turning 65.

MILLIONAIRES' GEOGRAPHY

The participants in the National Study of Millionaires were drawn from all 50 states and the District of Columbia. *Figure 3a* shows where the 2,000 randomly sampled participants in the quantitative phase live.

Figure 3a Geographic Distribution of Millionaires

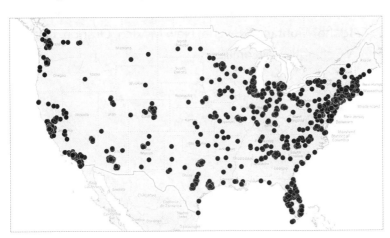

To further examine the millionaires in the study through a geo-graphical lens, the research team used a funnel design to process findings, beginning with broader geographic orientations and drilling down to more personal levels. For example, **Table 3b** shows the dis-tribution of participants from a regional perspective. The percentages indicate that distribution was essentially divided evenly across the four major regions recognized by the U.S. Census Bureau: Northeast (22%), Midwest (21%), South (29%) and West (28%). Each region includes the following states:

- **Northeast**: Connecticut, Maine, Massachusetts, New Hampshire, New Jersey, New York, Pennsylvania, Rhode Island, Vermont
- **Midwest**: Illinois, Indiana, Iowa, Kansas, Michigan, Minnesota, Missouri, Nebraska, North Dakota, Ohio, South Dakota, Wisconsin
- **South**: Alabama, Arkansas, Delaware, Florida, Georgia, Kentucky, Louisiana, Maryland, Mississippi, North Carolina, Oklahoma, South Carolina, Tennessee, Texas, Virginia, West Virginia[1]
- **West**: Alaska, Arizona, California, Colorado, Hawaii, Idaho, Montana, Nevada, New Mexico, Oregon, Utah, Washington, Wyoming

Table 3b Geographic Regions of Millionaires

Region	Millionaires	U.S. Census	Difference
Northeast	22%	17%	+5%
Midwest	21%	21%	0%
South	29%	38%	-9%
West	28%	24%	+4%

When compared to the distribution of the general population of the United States, three of the four regions demonstrated relatively similar levels of representation. The comparative distribution in the Midwest was essentially even, while the West (+4%) and the Northeast (+5%) showed slight overrepresentation of the random sample of millionaires. The one significant difference was found in the South, where 38% of the nation's general population lives. However, only 29% of the millionaires who participated in this study live in the South (-9%).

Moving down the funnel from a regional comparison to state distribution, *Table 3c* shows the states in which the concentration of the study's random sample of net-worth millionaires is highest when compared to the general population. Or stated another way, these are the states in which more millionaires live than is statistically expected based on the distribution of the nation's general population.

Table 3c Top 10 Millionaire States by Population Index

Rank	State	% of Millionaires	% of US Population
1	Arizona	3.78%	2.15%
2	Connecticut	1.92%	1.10%
3	Vermont	0.33%	0.19%
4	Hawaii	0.73%	0.44%
5	Massachusetts	3.05%	2.11%
6	Maryland	2.58%	1.86%
7	Illinois	5.37%	3.93%
8	New Jersey	3.71%	2.76%
9	Colorado	2.25%	1.72%
10	Minnesota	2.19%	1.71%

So, for example, approximately 3.78% of all millionaires in the study's random sample live in Arizona. However, only 2.15% of the nation's general population lives in that state. Therefore, the concentration of Arizona millionaires in the random sample exceeds what might be expected given Arizona's percentage of the general population. This is true to varying degrees for every state on this list.

It should be stated again that the net-worth millionaire numbers on this table refer only to those who participated in the National Study of Millionaires. As such, care must be taken when attempting to extrapolate a given state's universal population of millionaires. However, since the study used a representative random sample, it is reasonable to believe that the study's findings provide generally reliable information about the overall distribution of net-worth millionaires in each state.

In contrast to overrepresentation, **Table 3d** shows the other end of the millionaire spectrum. In these states, the concentration of the study's net-worth millionaires is much lower than what might be expected from the statistical distribution of the general population. While the overrepresented states were widely distributed, the underrepresented states appear to focus around the interior of the nation.

Table 3d Top 10 States Underrepresented by Millionaires

Rank	State	% of Millionaires	% of US Population
41	Tennessee	0.86%	2.06%
42	Montana	0.13%	0.32%
43	Alabama	0.60%	1.50%
44	Wyoming	0.07%	0.18%
45	West Virginia	0.20%	0.56%
46	Kentucky	0.46%	1.37%
47	South Dakota	0.07%	0.27%
48	Oklahoma	0.27%	1.21%
49	Mississippi	0.13%	0.92%
50	Idaho	0.07%	0.53%

Moving another level down the funnel, the research team examined the distribution of the study's net-worth millionaires by zip code. The research produced the following distribution:

- **Urban/Large Metropolitan**: 22%
- **Suburban/Residential**: 63%
- **Rural/Small Town**: 15%

These numbers seem to validate the thesis that a vast majority of net-worth millionaires are everyday people who live "normal" lives. Instead of living in fancy townhouses or condominiums in big cities, most of these individuals and their families live in the suburbs—close to, but clearly outside, large urban areas. To use Dr. Thomas Stanley's terminology, they are still "millionaires next door."

These findings are further validated in ***Figure 3e***. Drilling down to what could be considered a street level, Chris Hogan and the research team discovered that the net-worth millionaires in this study live in relatively modest homes located in ordinary neighborhoods. The U.S. Census Bureau states that the average square footage of the new American home is around 2,660 square feet.[2] The National Study of Millionaires found that the random sample's average home size is actually slightly smaller at 2,600 square feet.

Figure 3e Millionaires and Primary Residence

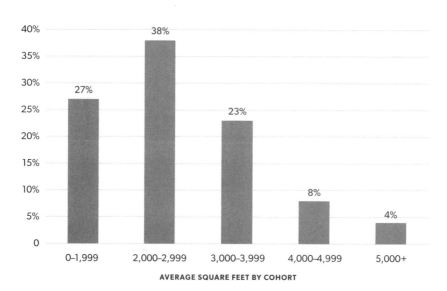

AVERAGE SQUARE FEET BY COHORT

When the participants' responses are broken down by category, two-thirds of net-worth millionaires (65%) live in a home that measures no more than 2,999 square feet. Another 23% have homes that are between 3,000–3,999 square feet. So, the majority of these millionaires and their families are not living in mansions or even larger homes.

In addition to modest homes, the zip code analysis suggests that the net-worth millionaires in this study also tend to live in modest neighborhoods. As **Figure 3f** demonstrates, more than half of these millionaires (51%) live in neighborhoods where the average family income is less than $75,000. This includes 16% who live in neighborhoods where the average family income is less than $50,000. Only one in five (21%) live in a neighborhood where the average family income exceeds $100,000.

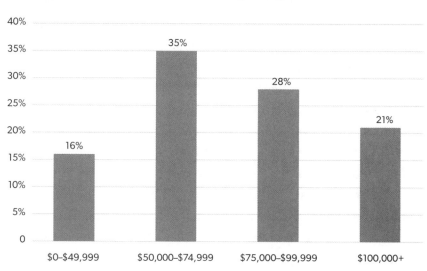

Figure 3f Millionaires and Average Neighborhood Income

MILLIONAIRES' FAMILY BACKGROUND

Family of origin has an incredible impact on the life of each individual. Understanding the power of someone's background can provide others with more insight into what that person does or believes. That being the case, Chris Hogan and the research team wanted to know more about the backstory of the everyday millionaires participating in the project. A summary of these findings from their childhood experiences is found below, along with information related to their educational achievements.

MILLIONAIRES' FAMILY

As noted elsewhere in the paper, few net-worth millionaires in the National Study of Millionaires received a substantial inheritance as they built wealth. One possible explanation for this can be found in *Figure 4a*. Among the participants in the study, only 21% came from upper-class or upper-middle-class families as defined by the U.S. Census Bureau. In contrast, approximately three out of every four (75%) were raised in families considered middle class or lower-middle class.

It is worth noting that more participants in the study came from lower-class families (4%) than from upper-class families (2%). In fact, nearly one out of every three participants in the study grew up in "working-class" families (lower class and lower-middle class), yet they managed to reach net-worth millionaire status. This finding supports the general belief that anyone can overcome obstacles and become an everyday millionaire.

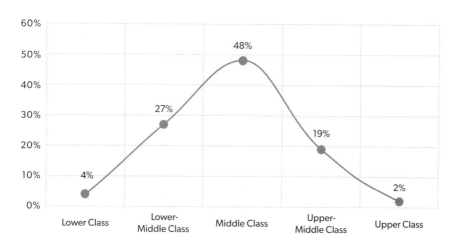

Figure 4a Income Class of Millionaires' Household During Childhood

Lower Class — 4%
Lower-Middle Class — 27%
Middle Class — 48%
Upper-Middle Class — 19%
Upper Class — 2%

Net-worth millionaires in the study also came from homes with a wide variety of parental education and occupations. As **Figure 4b** demonstrates, nearly half (47%) of the millionaires who took part in the survey came from homes where neither parent graduated from college or trade school. In contrast, only one in four came from homes where both parents earned a college degree.

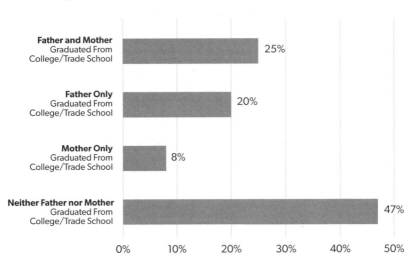

Figure 4b Education Level of Millionaires' Parents

Father and Mother Graduated From College/Trade School — 25%

Father Only Graduated From College/Trade School — 20%

Mother Only Graduated From College/Trade School — 8%

Neither Father nor Mother Graduated From College/Trade School — 47%

Likewise, the millionaires' parents pursued a variety of professions. The top five occupations of the parents include the following (in no particular order):

- Sales
- Small-Business Owner
- Engineer
- Farmer
- Accountant

The presence of engineers and accountants on this list indicates the rise of white-collar professions over time. The predominance of an agrarian society began its decline several decades ago, and the impact has been seen in the evolution of nonagricultural jobs.

But the transition was not complete during the childhood years of many everyday millionaires. Farmers are still present in the list, indicating that agriculture still had a powerful impact on the early lives of many net-worth millionaires. In addition, it may be argued that sales and small-business ownership looked much different during the millionaires' childhoods than they do today. For many, someone in sales worked in a smaller local store or sold items door to door. Likewise, small businesses dotted the landscape of small-town America a few decades ago. Instead of the fast-paced technology start-up, many entrepreneurs in that generation served their communities as tailors, butchers, barbers, grocers and florists.

MILLIONAIRES' EDUCATION

When examining their own academic histories, the net-worth millionaires in the National Study of Millionaires again paint a picture of ordinary lives. As *Figure 5a* shows, more than a third of the millionaires in the study were B students, while one in 10 were C students. These results indicate that while the millionaires were generally solid students in high school, their performance was typical of other students.

Figure 5a Millionaires and Type of Student

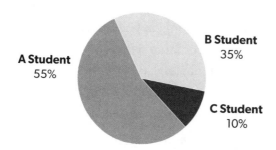

A Student
55%

B Student
35%

C Student
10%

In further support of this "average" lifestyle, *Figure 5b* shows that most of the study's millionaires (78%) were involved in extracurricular opportunities during their high school years. Sports and cheerleading provide the largest response in the research at 40%, but other categories are also well-represented. Service clubs (20%), student council (18%), academic teams (17%), band (17%) and the school newspaper (15%) were all reported by at least 15% of participants.

Figure 5b Millionaires and High School Extracurricular Activities

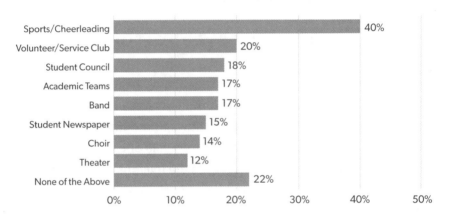

After high school, a vast majority of everyday millionaires moved on to receive some level of college education. As *Figure 5c* reveals, only 2% of net-worth millionaires stopped their formal education with a high school diploma or GED, while another 8% took some college classes without getting a degree. A few (3%) graduated with a two-year degree, but most millionaires in the study earned either a four-year bachelor's degree (36%) or graduate degree (38%). More than one in 10 (13%) went on to receive a doctorate.

Figure 5c Millionaires and Level of Education

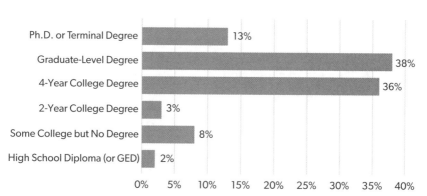

As noted above, many of these net-worth millionaires came from homes where neither parent earned a college degree. In fact, 46% of the millionaires in the study were first-generation college graduates. Their academic success also demonstrates a higher level of education than is found in the general population. While 51% of everyday millionaires earned a master's degree or doctorate, only 4% of the general population did the same.

Net-worth millionaires studied a variety of majors during their college experiences. While several pursued degrees in the business field, the sciences were also represented, along with education. *Table 5d* shows an alphabetic list of the top 10 degrees earned by participants in the National Study of Millionaires:

Table 5d Top 10 Degrees Earned in College

Accounting	Education
Biology	Engineering
Business Administration	Finance
Computer Science	Political Science
Economics	Psychology

As Chris Hogan noted in *Everyday Millionaires*, 62% of participants in the study attended public state universities. In addition, only 7% averaged more than $200,000 a year over the course of their careers. So, the research indicates that high-end educations and high-paying jobs are not the route most participants in the study took to reach net-worth millionaire status. Instead, they appear to be primarily normal people with normal backgrounds pursuing normal careers. Rather than experiencing overnight success, they are common folks who worked uncommonly hard over time to reach their goals.

MILLIONAIRES' NET WORTH

By definition, all the participants in the National Study of Millionaires had a seven-figure net worth. As noted, this was calculated by adding the value of all assets and subtracting the value of all liabilities. Assets included things such as homes, vehicles, investments, retirement accounts and savings accounts. Liabilities included credit card debt, lines of credit, car loans, student loans and personal loans.

The median net worth for all the net-worth millionaires in the study was $2,485,000. *Figure 6a* provides a breakdown of the millionaires in the study based on net worth. Nearly two-thirds (61%)

have a net worth of less than $3 million, including 33% with a net worth between $1–2 million. Approximately one in 10 study participants have a net worth exceeding $5 million.

Figure 6a Total Net Worth of Millionaire Study Participants

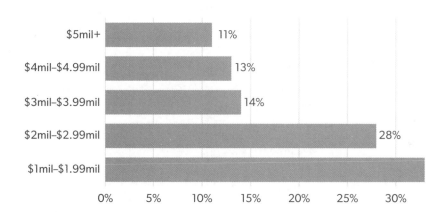

Of course, this does not represent future growth. It is possible that study participants could continue growing their wealth and move into higher net-worth brackets in the years to come.

Along with measuring their net worth, participants were asked about factors that contributed to achieving this wealth. Likewise, members of the randomly sampled general population group were asked about factors they perceived as helping net-worth millionaires reach that status.

As **Table 6b** and **Table 6c** show, both groups agreed that financial discipline is the most important factor in building a million-dollar net-worth portfolio and that real estate investments were the least important factor. However, millionaires and the general population diverge greatly from there.

	Table 6b			Table 6c	
	Millionaires and Building Wealth			General Population and Building Wealth	

Millionaires	Contributing Factor		General Population	Contributing Factor
1	Financial Discipline		1	Financial Discipline
2	Investment Consistency		2	Inheritance
3	Values From Upbringing		3	Investment Strategy
4	High-Paying Job		4	Luck
5	Investment Strategy		5	High-Paying Job
6	Luck		6	Values From Upbringing
7	Inheritance		7	Investment Consistency
8	Real Estate Investments		8	Real Estate Investments

Net-worth millionaires in the study stated that investment consistency was the second most important factor in building financial independence, while the general population believes it is only the seventh (out of eight) most important element. Likewise, the millionaires did not place as much value on inheritance (seventh of eight in their list), while the general population felt it was very important (second of eight). Non-millionaires also indicated that luck was relatively important (fourth), while the millionaires ranked it lower on the list (sixth).

In general, the responses indicate that millionaires tend to focus more on elements within an individual's control, while non-millionaires believe financial independence depends on elements outside of an individual's control.

In addition to examining factors necessary to create financial independence, researchers also asked participants about factors that could prevent an individual from reaching millionaire status. **Table 6d** and **Table 6e** provide the breakdown of those responses and reaffirm the differences between how millionaires view building wealth and how the general population views building wealth.

<table>
<tr><td colspan="2" align="center">**Table 6d**
Millionaires and
Preventing Wealth</td><td colspan="2" align="center">**Table 6e**
General Population and
Preventing Wealth</td></tr>
<tr><td>**Millionaires**</td><td>**Contributing Factor**</td><td>**General Population**</td><td>**Contributing Factor**</td></tr>
<tr><td>1</td><td>Lack of Financial Discipline</td><td>1</td><td>Lack of Financial Discipline</td></tr>
<tr><td>2</td><td>Consumerism</td><td rowspan="2">2</td><td rowspan="2">Lack of Opportunity</td></tr>
<tr><td>3</td><td>Low-Paying Jobs</td></tr>
<tr><td>4</td><td>Debt Levels</td><td>3</td><td>Low-Paying Jobs</td></tr>
<tr><td rowspan="2">5</td><td rowspan="2">Lack of Opportunity</td><td>4</td><td>Debt Levels</td></tr>
<tr><td>5</td><td>Cost of Living</td></tr>
<tr><td>6</td><td>Cost of Living</td><td>6</td><td>Consumerism</td></tr>
</table>

While both groups agreed that a lack of financial discipline makes it most difficult to find financial independence, the study's net-worth millionaires rated consumerism as the second greatest concern. In contrast, members of the general population ranked consumerism at the bottom of their list. Non-millionaires were also concerned about a lack of opportunity (second), which net-worth millionaires ranked only fifth.

As with the rankings of factors that help create wealth, the responses related to what hinders financial independence reflect a difference of attitude among net-worth millionaires in the study and their counterparts in the general population. The study revealed that personal responsibility and diligence were important priorities to the millionaires, so any factor that could derail such internal motivation was seen as a threat to building wealth. Meanwhile, those in the general population indicated that wealth was the product of external forces working on behalf of an individual, so anything that removes those factors from the equation is viewed as an obstacle.

UNDERSTANDING BEHAVIORS, CHARACTERISTICS AND MINDSET

IDENTIFYING THEMES FROM THE RESEARCH

As noted, the research began with qualitative interviews of more than 50 randomly sampled millionaires from around the country. The information gathered from those interviews was analyzed by the research team to identify common themes and topics that could be explored further in the quantitative phases.

After the interviews and analysis were complete, Hogan and the other team members identified seven major research themes for the quantitative phases. Each of these themes contrasted one action or attitude that helped individuals reach net-worth millionaire status with a corresponding action or attitude that did not. It was determined that each of these themes could be integrated into the survey questionnaire and could provide statistically significant data points.

1. **Proactive vs. Reactive**. Based on the research, millionaires tend to be planners and goal-setters. They view things from a long-term

perspective, which allows them to weather short-term storms. For example, they understand that saving today is difficult but produces greater benefits in the future. Rather than reacting to people or circumstances in the moment, net-worth millionaires stick to proven principles that keep them moving toward the goals they set.

2. **Earned vs. Inherited**. The vast majority of millionaires are self-made individuals. While the stereotype assumes that they were raised in prosperous families, the research indicates that most came from humble beginnings and worked hard over time. Instead of an inheritance, they gained net-worth millionaire status through disciplined saving over time and a commitment to lifelong learning. They rely on patience and persistence—not a silver spoon.

3. **Deciding vs. Sliding**. Millionaires in this study demonstrated intentionality with their resources. They chose to "happen" to their money instead of letting their money happen to them. They placed high value on decision-making skills and were convinced that nothing productive—including wealth—ever happens by accident. Even after becoming millionaires, they may appear countercultural. Their habits create greater financial independence, so they refuse to "slide" along following conventional wisdom.

4. **Coachable vs. Proud/Arrogant**. Millionaires recognize that they do not have all the answers and probably never will. As a result, they are committed to lifelong learning. If they have a question, they are not afraid to seek out the wisdom of someone who has the proper answer. Whether this involves a mentor figure or a professional advisor, millionaires are willing to listen and to use that

information to evaluate themselves. Because they are self-aware, millionaires are generally quick to admit their mistakes and to course correct when necessary.

5. **Living Modestly vs. Displaying Wealth**. More than two decades ago, Dr. Thomas Stanley introduced the idea of a "millionaire next door." That is, millionaires are more likely to be a neighbor or coworker than a flashy celebrity. The millionaires in this study demonstrated an aversion to extravagance. Their cars and their homes remain modest. In addition, they continue practicing many of the frugal habits that helped them reach net-worth millionaire status: budgeting, using coupons and grocery lists, shopping at discount or second-hand stores, and so forth.

6. **Growth Mindset vs. Fixed Mindset**. Stanford University researcher Dr. Carol Dweck has defined two contrasting mindsets that distinguish people.[3] The first is a fixed mindset through which intelligence is viewed as static. As a result, emphasis is placed on appearing to know something more than actually gaining the knowledge. The second is a growth mindset in which intelligence is constantly developing. As a result, emphasis is placed on continuing to learn and grow. Millionaires tend to demonstrate a growth mindset. Motivated to learn, they accept challenges and overcome obstacles. They develop perseverance. Most importantly, they recognize that embracing an opportunity does not limit the potential of others. To them, opportunities to learn and excel are like candles that can be used to light other candles—not pieces of pie that are gone once consumed.

---

[3] Carol S. Dweck, Ph.D., *Mindset: The New Psychology of Success* (New York: Ballantine Books, 2007).

7. **Owning It vs. Being a Victim**. Based on this research, millionaires take responsibility for their actions and their outcomes. Rather than being carried along by factors outside their control, the participants in this study made it clear that they were the masters of their own destiny. They rejected a victim mentality and were convinced that their success was determined primarily by their own choices and behaviors. As a result, they were convinced that any person could become a millionaire if that person was willing to make the sacrifices now that ensure a secure future.

CREATING AN ASSESSMENT TO VERIFY QUALITATIVE THEMES

As the research team analyzed these seven themes, a 30-question assessment was developed to better understand the findings and verify them in the field. The assessment focused on three broad topics that encompass the specific characteristics of wealth building demonstrated by the millionaires in the study. These topics were based on the seven themes identified in the qualitative interviews.

The topics are defined by three specific terms: behavior, knowledge and mindset. Behavior corresponds to the physical habits that most millionaires weave into their lives to ensure financial independence. These habits may be daily, weekly or even yearly, but they create regular wins that provide exponential growth over time.

Knowledge corresponds to the millionaires' desire to be lifelong learners. As noted above, the individuals in this study are committed to breaking free from the status quo and to improving over time. They have a desire to learn from mentors and other resources and are not afraid of challenges and obstacles. Most importantly, learning is not an end unto itself; it provides the path for making positive changes in their lives.

Mindset corresponds to the emotional qualities that millionaires see as important to their growth and future stability. These are defined by their core values and principles—the nonnegotiable elements that serve as the foundation for their world view. Mindset also includes elements such as discipline and the will to take necessary steps toward reaching a goal. This provides the belief and confidence that they could become net-worth millionaires and is the basis for their conviction that others can follow the same path toward success.

Understanding these three areas should reveal habits and traits that make millionaires unique. If net-worth millionaire status is the result of hard work and discipline—in contrast to inheritances or luck— it's worth noting that time is also a key principle that cannot be ignored. Time and patience stand at the heart of building wealth.

DESIGNING THE ASSESSMENT

Once the themes were identified, the research team worked to determine how to integrate them into the quantitative research. The key was to imbed a series of relevant statements related to the qualitative themes within the larger body of the survey questionnaire. This allowed researchers to gain useful information about each of the three areas without creating a negative impact on the rest of the study.

Thirty statements were included in the 119 questions of the larger survey instrument. This 30-statement assessment included statements evenly divided between behaviors, knowledge and mindsets of millionaires. Researchers used a five-point Likert scale format that ranged from "strongly disagree" to "strongly agree." The statements provided weighted averages for each response, with more weight assigned to the higher end of the Likert scale.

In addition to distributing this 30-statement assessment as part of the questionnaire for the random white space sampling of the study, the 2,000 individuals in the general population phase also received the same survey and provided responses. As a result, researchers were able to measure the differences between millionaire perspectives and non-millionaire perspectives on the seven themes and the three areas of study.

The responses, along with comparisons to the general population, will be discussed in the following sections. In these comparisons, anything generally falling within the range of +/-2 was considered "neutral." Anything falling between +3 and +9 was considered "somewhat positive," and anything at +10 or above was considered "positive."

At times, due to specific wording structures, some statements were considered "positive" when the results provided a low or negative correlation. Those exceptions will be noted and explained below.

BEHAVIOR RESPONSES

As noted, 10 of the 30 Likert-style statements in the survey instrument related to the behavior and habits of millionaires. *Table 7a* shows the responses to one set of behavior-related statements provided by the 2,000 millionaires in the random white space phase of the study. This set of statements represents five of the 10 statements related to behavior.

Table 7a Weighted Averages for Behavior Statements, Set 1

BEHAVIOR Statements, Set 1	Millionaires	Median	StdDv
I have a long-term plan for my money	4.42	5.00	0.69
I plan for upcoming expenses by saving in advance	4.30	4.00	0.84
I live on less money than I make	4.35	5.00	0.92
I never carry a balance on my credit card	4.70	5.00	0.77
I stick to the budgets I create	3.85	4.00	0.91

As the weighted averages indicate, the responses of the participants to four of the five statements skew very close to "strongly agree." The one exception was a statement about budgets, which still garnered a 3.85, which was closer to "agree." The median score of 4.00 also indicates a strong measure of agreement with the statement in general.

One of the primary findings from this set related to the fourth statement about credit card balances. The weighted average of 4.70 represents the highest average for any statement in the assessment. The result indicates that avoiding consumer debt, specifically balances on credit cards, is one action millionaires believe will lead to financial independence.

As noted, the questionnaire, including the 30-statement assessment, was also distributed to a random sample of 2,000 general population participants. The comparisons between the two groups on this five-statement set are found in *Table 7b*.

Table 7b General Population Comparison
for Behavior Statements, Set 1

BEHAVIOR Statements, Set 1	General Population	Median	StdDv
I have a long-term plan for my money	3.62	4.00	1.13
I plan for upcoming expenses by saving in advance	3.77	4.00	1.07
I live on less money than I make	3.49	4.00	1.18
I never carry a balance on my credit card	3.36	4.00	1.51
I stick to the budgets I create	3.49	4.00	1.02

Across this set, the millionaires' responses demonstrated a positive correlation when compared to the general population. For example, the 4.70 weighted average on the credit card balance statement was 40% higher than the weighted average of the general population. Even the lower 3.85 average on the budgeting statement showed a positive correlation (+10%) when compared to the general population. In scoring higher on five out of five statements, the results indicate that millionaires are more likely to participate in these actions than the average American.

Table 8a shows the responses to the five remaining behavior-related statements. While the weighted averages for these responses are not as large as the first Behavior set, they still fall within "agree." The highest average (4.21 for the fifth statement in the set) indicates that net-worth millionaires are highly motivated and demonstrate perseverance over time. They are determined to complete a task once it has been started.

Table 8a Weighted Averages for Behavior Statements, Set 2

BEHAVIOR Statements, Set 2	Millionaires	Median	StdDv
I set aside some of my income every month to give to others	3.47	4.00	1.19
I regularly set personal goals and often write them down	3.11	3.00	1.15
I read approximately one nonfiction book a month	2.88	3.00	1.34
I almost always achieve my goals	3.92	4.00	0.72
If I start something, I finish it	4.21	4.00	0.70

The lowest weighted average for this set involves the habit of reading (2.88), but the median for that statement (3.00) still indicates that an "average" net-worth millionaire (half are, half aren't) is reading a book a month and sees it as an important habit for finding success. This correlates with both the "coachable" and "growth mindset" themes, which emphasize lifelong learning.

The information in *Table 8b* generally shows positive correlation for the millionaires, as once again, they score higher than the general population on four out of five statements. The weighted averages demonstrate that while millionaires write down goals, the general population is about as likely to do the same. Millionaires are more likely than the general population to read at least one nonfiction book each month (+12%). The millionaires also are much more intentional about giving and generosity than the general population (+19%).

Table 8b General Population Comparison for Behavior Statements, Set 2

BEHAVIOR Statements, Set 2	General Population	Median	StdDv
I set aside some of my income every month to give to others	2.92	3.00	1.22
I regularly set personal goals and often write them down	3.11	3.00	1.12
I read approximately one nonfiction book a month	2.57	2.00	1.27
I almost always achieve my goals	3.61	4.00	0.90
If I start something, I finish it	3.90	4.00	0.88

In general, the research reveals that millionaires place a great deal of value on particular habits that they believe will ensure their financial independence. When compared to the general population, these net-worth millionaires are more likely to practice these habits than those who have not reached millionaire status.

MINDSET RESPONSES

Table 9a shows the responses to one set of statements reflective of a person's mindset. As with the Behavior statements, the net-worth millionaires in the random white space sample demonstrated high levels of agreement and strong agreement in these statements.

Table 9a Weighted Averages for Mindset Statements, Set 1

MINDSET Statements, Set 1	Millionaires	Median	StdDv
My friends and family would say I am disciplined	4.29	4.00	0.69
My friends and family would describe me as a hard worker	4.34	4.00	0.70
I do what I think is best, regardless of other people's opinions	4.22	4.00	0.70
At times, I get jealous of my friends/family because of the things they have or get to do	2.14	2.00	1.09
I keep my promises and meet my commitments	4.47	5.00	0.62

With one exception (which will be noted below), the weighted averages for these statements ranged from 4.22 ("I do what I think is best, regardless of other people's opinions") to 4.47 ("I keep my promises and meet my commitments"). As noted, the mindset statements allowed the Ramsey team to dig into the core values and principles that motivate net-worth millionaires. These weighted averages indicate that participants hold qualities such as integrity, honesty, hard work, discipline, reliability and self-determination in high standing.

The one exception from this set relates to feelings of personal jealousy (weighted average of 2.14). This statement represented an "attention filter" for participants. As a best practice, the research team included statements for which the proper response ranked lower ("disagree" or "strongly disagree") on the Likert scale. This ensures that those surveyed are paying attention and not just marking every response high.

In this case, it is expected that millionaires with a proper perspective do not struggle with feelings of jealousy toward friends and family. A "keeping up with the Joneses" mentality can be detrimental to one's personal finance journey. As a result, the expected responses were rated lower ("disagree" and "strongly disagree") on the Likert scale. Both the weighted averages and the median scores provided by the net-worth millionaires in this study showed that they were properly engaged with the statements on the survey instrument *and* that jealousy was not an issue with a majority of participants.

The information in **Table 9b** again shows a generally positive correlation for net-worth millionaires when compared to the general population. The weighted averages indicate that millionaires may view the virtue of discipline as a stronger motivational factor than do non-millionaires (+10%).

Table 9b General Population Comparison
for Mindset Statements, Set 1

MINDSET Statements, Set 1	General Population	Median	StdDv
My friends and family would say I am disciplined	3.91	4.00	0.89
My friends and family would describe me as a hard worker	4.18	4.00	0.83
I do what I think is best, regardless of other people's opinions	4.01	4.00	0.83
At times, I get jealous of my friends/family because of the things they have or get to do	2.67	3.00	1.22
I keep my promises and meet my commitments	4.19	4.00	0.80

The same could also be said to a lesser—but still meaningful—degree of hard work (+4%), self-determination (+5%) and reliability (+7%). So, while both the millionaires and the general population agree that these factors are important, the net-worth millionaires are more likely to connect them to personal success—including financial independence—than non-millionaires.

It should be noted that the "attention filter" related to jealousy demonstrated a positive correlation for the net-worth millionaires. Since a response on the lower end of the Likert scale represented a healthy perspective, a lower weighted average is considered desirable. With this in mind, the -20% correlation is actually quite positive for the millionaires, indicating that they are much less likely to feel jealousy toward others than members of the general population.

Table 10a shows the responses to the second set of statements related to the area of Mindset. As with the second set of Behavior statements, the weighted averages for these responses are somewhat lower than the first set of Mindset statements. However, they generally do represent a significant level of agreement with the values under consideration.

Table 10a Weighted Averages for Mindset Statements, Set 2

MINDSET Statements, Set 2	Millionaires	Median	StdDv
With hard work and discipline, anyone can become a millionaire	3.59	4.00	1.11
My friends and family would say I am thrifty	3.91	4.00	0.95
I feel pressure to keep up with my friends and family when it comes to money	1.86	2.00	0.92
I am willing to sacrifice to win— even when it's painful	3.16	3.00	1.02
I control my own destiny and am responsible for my future	4.22	4.00	0.76

While its weighted average registered lower than other responses, the virtue of personal sacrifice (3.16) still rated above average among net-worth millionaires. The millionaires in the study also affirmed hard work (3.59) and thrift (3.91). The strongest weighted average was related to the statement on self-determination. At 4.22, the millionaires demonstrated a strong reliance on personal responsibility, which indicates a refusal to succumb to a "victim mentality" of any kind. It could be said that they believe in themselves and their own ability to "happen" to life instead of passively allowing things to happen to them.

The statement related to keeping up with the standards of others served as another attention filter for participants. As explained earlier, a response lower on the Likert scale is expected for this statement. So, the weighted average of 1.86 indicates a healthy aversion to what might commonly be called "keeping up with the Joneses." Millionaires tend to define success on their own terms—not by what others around them think or do.

The information in **Table 10b** compares the weighted averages for the net-worth millionaire sample to the responses drawn from the general population sample. In these comparisons, millionaires had the strongest positive correlations on the topics of thrift (+10%) and hard work/discipline (+14%). The research responses showed moderate positive correlation for self-determination (+6%).

Table 10b General Population Comparison
for Mindset Statements, Set 2

MINDSET Statements, Set 2	General Population	Median	StdDv
With hard work and discipline, anyone can become a millionaire	3.15	3.00	1.18
My friends and family would say I am thrifty	3.56	4.00	1.06
I feel pressure to keep up with my friends and family when it comes to money	2.43	2.00	1.18
I am willing to sacrifice to win—even when it's painful	3.20	3.00	1.03
I control my own destiny and am responsible for my future	3.99	4.00	0.90

The statement addressing personal sacrifice proved to be one of the few examples of a neutral or negative correlation of millionaires to the general population. The weighted averages of both groups indicate that non-millionaires are slightly more willing to endure sacrifices in the short term if it means success in the long term.

Again, the large difference related to the attention filter ("I feel pressure to keep up with my friends and family when it comes to money") actually represents a positive correlation for the net-worth millionaires. The results show that millionaires are 23% less likely to feel pressured to keep up with others. Stated positively, they are much more likely to define their success by their own standards, not the standards of others.

KNOWLEDGE RESPONSES

Table 11a shows the responses to the first set of statements correlated to the area of Knowledge. In general, the weighted averages for the Knowledge set were lower than those of the Behavior or Mindset groupings. However, as the median scores reveal, most millionaires "agree" that the qualities and characteristics included in this subset are valuable for building wealth and finding financial independence and show separation between themselves and the general population.

Table 11a Weighted Averages for Knowledge Statements, Set 1

KNOWLEDGE Statements, Set 1	Millionaires	Median	StdDv
I accept and integrate feedback from others	3.91	4.00	0.63
There are some things I am not capable of learning	2.70	4.00	1.07
I will try difficult things to get new results	3.77	4.00	0.72
Challenging myself won't make me any smarter	2.28	2.00	0.92
I am always trying to learn new things	3.93	4.00	0.74

In this first five-statement Knowledge set, the weighted averages tended to hover around "agree" as observed by the median scores. In some instances, though, the research team reverse coded responses, meaning "strongly disagree" and "disagree" were given the greater weight. This method was used for statements stated as negatives to which respondents were expected to respond using the lower end of the Likert scale.

For example, the second statement in the set ("There are some things I am not capable of learning") is stated as a negative, so it is expected that millionaires would provide answers that correlate to the low end of the Likert scale ("strongly disagree" or "disagree"). The weighted average of 2.70 reveals that net-worth millionaires are confident (but not arrogant) in regard to their ability to gain new information and learning. This is key to building wealth, as one rarely "has it all figured out."

Likewise, the fourth statement in the set ("Challenging myself won't make me any smarter") is stated in the negative, so a lower response is most healthy and positive. Therefore, the weighted average of 2.28 indicates that the net-worth millionaires in the study are essentially confident that they can gain knowledge when appropriately challenged. Many individuals seek to avoid challenges, but millionaires are typically receptive to challenges because they see difficult circumstances a means of growth and a path to greater success.

In contrast, the first statement ("I accept and integrate feedback from others") and the third statement ("I am always trying to learn new things") are worded positively. As a result, Hogan and the team expected responses that ranked higher on the Likert scale. Millionaires responded as expected, producing the highest weighted averages in the set at 3.91 and 3.93, respectively.

Table 11b shows a somewhat lower positive correlation between net-worth millionaires and the general population. The largest difference between the groups can be found in the weighted average of the second statement ("There are some things I am not capable of learning"). Again, the average of -13% indicates that the millionaires are much more likely to believe they can continue learning throughout life than the general population. This provides a positive correlation when the millionaires are compared to the non-millionaires.

Table 11b General Population Comparison for Knowledge Statements, Set 1

KNOWLEDGE Statements, Set 1	General Population	Median	StdDv
I accept and integrate feedback from others	3.78	4.00	0.76
There are some things I am not capable of learning	3.09	3.00	1.10
I will try difficult things to get new results	3.66	4.00	0.83
Challenging myself won't make me any smarter	2.40	2.00	1.03
I am always trying to learn new things	3.90	4.00	0.83

In the same way, the -5% correlation found in the fourth statement ("Challenging myself won't make me any smarter") is a positive correlation for millionaires. The weighted averages reveal that net-worth millionaires are less likely to believe challenges will not help them grow than participants in the general population. Or, stated as a positive, they are more likely to believe that the challenges of life provide valuable learning experiences that can lead them toward financial success.

The responses for the statements related to integrating feedback, trying difficult things, and learning new things could all be considered "somewhat positive" correlations for millionaires compared to non-millionaires.

Table 12a shows the responses to the second set of statements related to Knowledge and the final set of statements in the 30-item assessment. As with the previous Knowledge set, the weighted averages are somewhat lower than in the Behavior and Mindset groupings, but in general, the medians still point toward agreement.

Table 12a Weighted Averages for Knowledge Statements, Set 2

KNOWLEDGE Statements, Set 2	Millionaires	Median	StdDv
I am willing to be wrong and quickly admit to it	3.86	4.00	0.71
My intelligence is something that I can't change very much	2.29	3.00	1.09
If I am not naturally smart in a subject, I will never do well in it	2.41	2.00	0.92
I seek out wisdom from mentors	3.67	4.00	0.86
I am always trying to improve my habits	3.85	4.00	0.75

The first exception is found in the second statement of the set. As mentioned above in discussing the other sets, this statement ("My intelligence is something that I can't change very much") is presented as a negative and was reverse coded by the research team. A response from the lower end of the Likert scale is expected, and the millionaires responded with a weighted average of 2.29. This means that millionaires generally believe their intelligence has the potential to increase over time.

Similarly, the third statement in the set ("If I am not naturally smart in a subject, I will never do well in it") is negative and was reverse coded. The net-worth millionaires in the study provided a weighted average of 2.41, meaning they are confident that they can study and master information that was previously unfamiliar to them. Both of these statements are used to show a growth mindset among millionaires, rather than fixed.

The remaining weighted averages in this set are similar, and the median for each of these statements is 4.00. This indicates a high level of agreement on each subject.

Table 12b includes results that will look similar to the comparisons in other sets. The first and fifth statements produced "Somewhat Positive" correlations for net-worth millionaires when aligned with the corresponding responses from the general population. However, the fourth statement ("I seek out wisdom from mentors") produced a neutral correlation that slightly favored the general population. In simpler terms, the research found that members of the general population are perhaps more likely to rely on mentors than net-worth millionaires. But the difference between the two is not substantial.

Table 12b General Population Comparison for Knowledge Statements, Set 2

KNOWLEDGE Statements, Set 2	General Population	Median	StdDv
I am willing to be wrong and quickly admit to it	3.71	4.00	0.86
My intelligence is something that I can't change very much	2.69	3.00	1.07
If I am not naturally smart in a subject, I will never do well in it	2.50	2.00	1.00
I seek out wisdom from mentors	3.73	4.00	0.89
I am always trying to improve my habits	3.83	4.00	0.78

The second and third statements of the set follow the pattern of previous negatives. Millionaires rated those statements low on the Likert scale, and those responses were much lower than the responses provided by the general population. Therefore, the negative correlations (-17% for the second statement and -4% in the third) are interpreted as positive correlations for the millionaires.

CONCLUSIONS FROM THE ASSESSMENT

When all 30 statements in the assessment are considered, the weighted averages of the 2,000 randomly sampled net-worth millionaires were consistently higher than the corresponding scores from the random sampling of general population participants. In 27 of the 30 items, the millionaires ranked higher than the general population. Therefore, the research indicates that millionaires are more likely to practice specific behaviors, own particular beliefs, and thirst for the kind of knowledge that leads to financial independence and net-worth millionaire status.

In addition, **Figure 13** demonstrates high levels of agreement among millionaires on a vast majority of the 30 statements used in the assessment. Using a standard of 70% to define "agreement," the millionaires found strong common ground on 26 statements. In addition, they found agreement of at least 90% on 19 of the items.

This also takes into account the negatively worded statements for which agreement is defined as less than 30%. For example, only 7% of the millionaires agreed with the statement "I feel pressure to keep up with my friends and family when it comes to money." Researchers expect healthy individuals to "strongly disagree" or "disagree" with that statement, so a 93% disagreement rate is considered positive.

Three additional statements—related to sacrifice, personal goals and gaining intelligence—garnered at least 50% agreement among the millionaires. Only one statement ("I read approximately one non-fiction book a month") found slightly less than 50% agreement.

Figure 13 Agreement Among Net-Worth Millionaires
(continued on next page)

#	Hypothesis Test With Net-Worth Millionaires	% of Agreement
1	I have a long-term plan for my money	99%
2	My friends and family would describe me as a hard worker	99%
3	I keep my promises and meet my commitments	99%
4	If I start something, I finish it	98%
5	My friends and family would say I am disciplined	98%
6	I do what I think is best, regardless of other people's opinions	98%
7	I accept and integrate feedback from others	98%
8	I almost always achieve my goals	97%
9	I control my own destiny and am responsible for my future	97%
10	I never carry a balance on my credit card	96%
11	I am always trying to learn new things	96%
12	I plan for upcoming expenses by saving in advance	95%
13	I am willing to be wrong and quickly admit to it	95%
14	I live on less money than I make	94%
15	I will try difficult things to get new results	94%
16	I am always trying to improve my habits	94%
17	I feel pressure to keep up with my friends and family when it comes to money	7%
18	I stick to the budgets I create	93%
19	My friends and family would say I am thrifty	90%
20	Challenging myself won't make me any smarter	14%
21	I seek out wisdom from mentors	86%
22	At times, I get jealous of my friends/family because of the things they have or get to do	17%

Figure 13 Agreement Among Net-Worth Millionaires *(continued)*

#	Hypothesis Test With Net-Worth Millionaires	% of Agreement
23	If I am not naturally smart in a subject, I will never do well in it	18%
24	My intelligence is something that I can't change very much	18%
25	With hard work and discipline, anyone can become a millionaire	76%
26	I set aside some of my income every month to give to others	70%
27	There are some things I am not capable of learning	38%
28	I am willing to sacrifice to win—even when it's painful	61%
29	I regularly set personal goals and often write them down	55%
30	I read approximately one nonfiction book a month	45%

SOCIETAL BELIEFS ABOUT MILLIONAIRES

GENERAL POPULATION BELIEFS

In addition to examining the habits and attitudes that led individuals to become net-worth millionaires, Chris Hogan and the research team also wanted to dig deeper into the culture's underlying attitudes toward building wealth. To that end, the team created a list of 10 common beliefs that individuals express about wealthy people and the process of becoming wealthy. They then used a five-point Likert scale to measure the levels of agreement toward each belief within the general population.

Any response that received a majority of agreement (at least 50% of the general population) was considered a belief confirmed.

Figure 14 provides the agreement percentages for each of the 10 beliefs. Of the 10 statements, seven were confirmed by the general population. The most common belief related to the use of debt (86%), followed by the support of wealthy families (77%) and the need to take big risks to make money (67%).

Figure 14 Common Beliefs Around Building Wealth

#	Common Beliefs Around Building Wealth	General Population
1	Wealthy people use debt in their favor to make more money	86%
2	Most wealthy people come from wealthy families	77%
3	To become rich, you have to take big risks with your money	67%
4	The majority of millionaires inherited their money	62%
5	You need a six-figure salary to become a millionaire in today's economy	62%
6	Most millionaires have a million-dollar home	56%
7	You have to be lucky to get rich	51%
8	Wealthy people are materialistic, self-centered, obsessed with having more	45%
9	To become rich, you need to act rich	25%
10	If you're born into a poor family, you can't become wealthy	18%

Interestingly, two of the three statements that were not confirmed related to general perceptions about wealthy people. The general population essentially denied the beliefs that wealthy people are self-centered (45%) and try to act rich when they are not (25%). The lowest agreement rating was attached to the belief that individuals born into poor families cannot become wealthy (18%).

GENERAL POPULATION
COMPARED TO MILLIONAIRES

When comparing the general population's attitudes toward the responses of net-worth millionaires in the study, it becomes apparent that millionaires view the beliefs through a different lens. As **Figure 15b** demonstrates, the millionaires who participated in the research were less likely than the general population to agree with every statement on the list. Nine of the 10 belief statements drew less that 50% affirmation from the everyday millionaires in the study.

The differences in responses between millionaires and the general population created substantial gaps for most of the belief statements, as shown in **Figure 15a**. The largest differences between the two groups were found in the beliefs about takings big risks with money (51%) and the value of millionaires' homes (41%). Two other beliefs revealed a difference of at least 30%: Wealthy people come from wealthy families (39%), and most wealthy people inherit their money (31%).

Figure 15a
Differences in Wealth-Building Beliefs Between
General Population and Millionaires

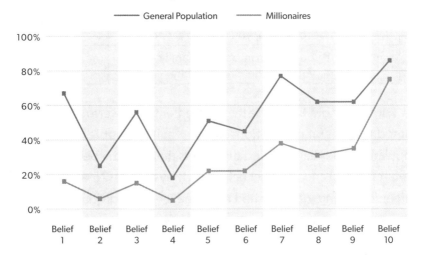

Table 15b Common Beliefs Comparison

Belief #	Common Beliefs and Differences in Agreement	General Popuation	Millionaires
1	To become rich, you have to take big risks with your money	67%	16%
2	To become rich, you need to act rich	25%	6%
3	Most millionaires have a million-dollar home	56%	15%
4	If you're born into a poor family, you can't become wealthy	18%	5%
5	You have to be lucky to get rich	51%	22%
6	Wealthy people are materialistic, self-centered, obsessed with having more	45%	22%
7	Most wealthy people come from wealthy families	77%	38%
8	The majority of millionaires inherited their money	62%	31%
9	You need a six-figure salary to become a millionaire in today's economy	62%	35%
10	Wealthy people use debt in their favor to make more money	86%	75%

In an interesting note, the lowest margins of disagreement were found on opposite ends of the spectrum. The smallest difference was rooted in the only belief that a majority of millionaires and the general population agreed upon: Using debt as a tool for building wealth (11%). The next smallest margin was found concerning the belief that produced the lowest level of agreement for both groups: Individuals from poor families cannot become millionaires (13%).

Another interesting finding from this data set is the response of everyday millionaires to the use of debt in building wealth. As noted above, this was the only belief that drew affirmation from a majority of net-worth millionaires in the study (75%). Yet, other parts of the study indicate that most of these millionaires have carefully avoided debt throughout their lives. Perhaps the best way to reconcile these two perspectives is to consider that while most millionaires have not personally used debt as a tool for building wealth, they may believe that other millionaires have relied on debt to reach their net-worth millionaire status.

GENERATIONAL BELIEFS

In addition to making general comparisons between net-worth millionaires and the general population, Chris Hogan and the research team also examined how societal beliefs about wealth played out across various generations. Specifically, the agreement levels for the belief statements were segmented across three broad groupings: Baby Boomers, Generation X and Millennials. In general, the range of reactions to the common beliefs was more widespread among the younger generations.

Figure 15c Differences in Wealth-Building Beliefs by Generation

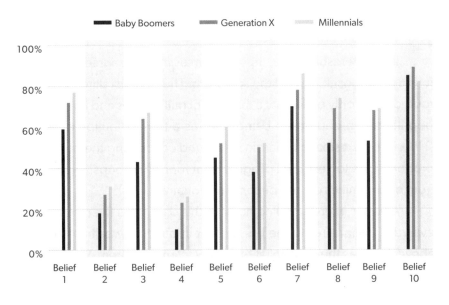

THE NATIONAL STUDY OF MILLIONAIRES

Table 15d Differences in Wealth-Building Beliefs by Generation

Belief #	Common Beliefs Around Building Wealth	Boomers	Gen X	Millennials
1	To become rich, you have to take big risks with your money	59%	72%	77%
2	To become rich, you need to act rich	18%	27%	31%
3	Most millionaires have a million-dollar home	43%	64%	67%
4	If you're born into a poor family, you can't become wealthy	10%	23%	26%
5	You have to be lucky to get rich	45%	52%	60%
6	Wealthy people are materialistic, self-centered, obsessed with having more money	38%	50%	52%
7	Most wealthy people come from wealthy families	70%	78%	86%
8	The majority of millionaires inherited their money	52%	69%	74%
9	You need a six-figure salary to become a millionaire in today's economy	53%	68%	69%
10	Wealthy people use debt in their favor to make more money	85%	89%	82%

As the bar graph on **Figure15c** indicates, the common beliefs measured in the study appear to become more entrenched in younger generations. For nine of the 10 belief statements, the percentages of agreement were higher for younger generations. For example, the belief that wealth comes from taking big risks with money was agreed upon by 59% of Baby Boomers, but that percentage was 72% for Generation X and 77% for Millennials. Similarly, while seven in 10 Baby Boomers believe that wealthy people come from wealthy families, the percentages among Generation X (78%) and Millennials (86%) are higher.

Along with this apparent skepticism about what millionaires did to build wealth, younger generations also demonstrated a more negative attitude toward net-worth millionaires in general. For instance, only 38% of Baby Boomers think wealthy people are "materialistic, self-centered, and obsessed with having more money." However, that percentage was 50% among members of Generation X and 52% among Millennials. Likewise, Generation X (27%) and Millennials (31%) are more likely to believe that people must act rich to get rich than Baby Boomers in the general population (18%).

The only belief statement that showed variance from this pattern was the final item on the list: "Wealthy people use debt in their favor to make more money." For this statement, 85% of the Baby Boomers in the general population agreed. That number was 89% for Generation X but only 82% for Millennials. **Table 15d** shows the information in numeric form.

Researchers might suggest two explanations (or a combination of them) for these findings. It might be said that younger generations have become more convinced of these beliefs and that they are more cynical than their elders when it comes to building wealth. However, it is also possible that older generations have more experience in building wealth and have discovered that these beliefs are not necessarily accurate. Their experiences make them less likely to affirm the beliefs than younger generations.

ADDITIONAL INSIGHTS FROM THE RESEARCH

A random sample of 2,000 net-worth millionaires responded to the 119-question survey instrument as part of the National Study of Millionaires. In addition, another 2,000 participants from a random sample of the general population responded to the survey.

Many of the top findings from this study can be found within the pages of *Everyday Millionaires*, published in January 2019 by Ramsey Press. However, this section of this white paper adds additional data, providing more information and insights into the research results. The six specific areas highlighted in this section include Millionaires and Debt, Millionaires and Saving, Millionaires and Spending, Millionaires and Cars, Millionaires and Building Wealth, and Millionaires and Inheritances.

MILLIONAIRES AND DEBT

The research revealed that net-worth millionaires typically avoid debt, especially when compared to the general population. To illustrate this point, **Table 16a** compares the percentages of individuals currently holding debt in both the random sample of 2,000 net-worth millionaires and the random sample drawn from the general population. In almost every category, millionaires are relying on debt much less frequently than non-millionaires.

Table 16a Current Debt Percentages

% Who Currently Hold the Following Debt	General Population	Millionaires
Credit Card Debt	40%	6%
Auto Loan	35%	18%
Student Loan	22%	2%
Medical Debt	12%	2%
Family/Friend Loan	8%	1%
Past-Due Utilities	8%	1%
Cash Advance	4%	1%
Business Loan	2%	2%
Home Equity Loan	9%	10%
Mortgage Loan	34%	30%

For example, 40% of the general population currently have credit card debt, compared to only 6% of net-worth millionaires. Likewise, non-millionaires are almost twice as likely to have outstanding car loans (35% compared to 18%) and nearly ten times more likely to be paying back student loans (22% compared to 2%).

One area in which the percentages for millionaires and the general population are similar is real estate. Millionaires are slightly more likely than non-millionaires to be carrying home equity loans (10% compared to 9%) and almost as likely to have a mortgage (30% for millionaires compared to 34% for the general population). This may be due to the fact that millionaires are more likely to participate in homeownership than non-millionaires. Also, it should be noted that unlike consumer debt, real estate tends to rise in value over time, making a mortgage less dangerous than other forms of debt.

Some might argue that net-worth millionaires inherently have less need of debt than members of the general population. Because they have attained financial independence, they do not have to rely on debt instruments, such as loans and credit cards. However, *Table 16b* indicates that, in general, net-worth millionaires have always avoided debt throughout the course of their lives—even before they became millionaires.

Table 16b Lifetime Debt Percentages

% Who Have *Ever* Held the Following Debt	General Population	Millionaires
Credit Card Debt	66%	27%
Student Loan	47%	29%
Family/Friend Loan	37%	19%
Past-Due Utilities	29%	4%
Cash Advance	17%	6%
Medical Debt	35%	7%
Auto Loan	73%	65%
Business Loan	8%	10%
Home Equity Loan	28%	37%
Mortgage Loan	62%	86%

For example, net-worth millionaires are more than twice as likely to have stayed away from credit card debt than the general population over time. Nearly three-fourths of all millionaires (73%) said they have *never* had credit card debt. Meanwhile, only 34% of the general population could say the same.

Likewise, only 4% of net-worth millionaires said they have ever paid a utility bill late, compared to almost one-third (29%) of the general population. And while nearly one-half of non-millionaires have taken out student loans (47%), less than a third of millionaires (29%) ever borrowed money to pay for college.

Again, the percentage of millionaires who have held home equity loans or mortgages is higher than the general population. But, as noted, this might be attributed to the number of net-worth millionaires who actually own their homes compared to non-millionaires.

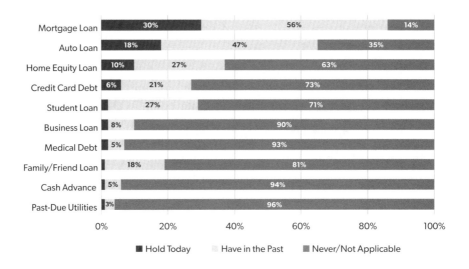

Figure 16c Millionaires and Debt (Full Data)
Which of these debts do you hold today or have you held in the past?

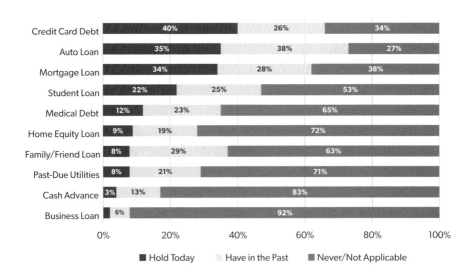

Figure 16d General Population and Debt (Full Data)
Which of these debts do you hold today or have you held in the past?

MILLIONAIRES AND SAVING

As noted earlier, most everyday millionaires surveyed in the National Study of Millionaires did not inherit the bulk of their wealth. Any money they may have received from their families was not enough to establish a million-dollar net worth. In fact, many essentially built their wealth from scratch after being raised on low- to moderate-income families.

This being the case, it is reasonable to assume that at some point in life these net-worth millionaires learned the value of saving money. The research indicates that this includes applying discipline to set money aside for the future through savings accounts or investment tools. But it also involves saving money in the present through budgeting and other habits.

Saving for the Future. In general, net-worth millionaires can be classified as "savers." The everyday millionaires who took part in the National Study of Millionaires follow that pattern in their own lives. As shown in **Figure 17a**, only 3% of the net-worth millionaires in the research reported that they set nothing aside in savings each month.

Figure 17a Millionaires and Percentage of Income Saved per Month

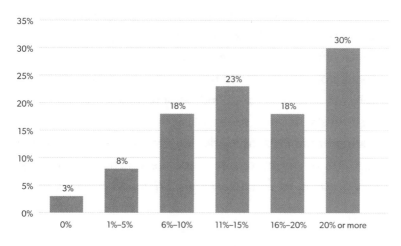

Nearly half (48%) of the net-worth millionaires questioned said they save at least 16% of their income each month, including 30% who save at least 20% of their income. In fact, almost nine out of 10 participants (89%) set aside at least 6% each month.

These numbers suggest at least two important implications for net-worth millionaires. First, such commitment to saving underscores the importance of regular saving as a tool for reaching net-worth millionaire status. Saving money not only provides security in the present through the presence of an emergency fund, but it also primes the pump for investments that build wealth over time. Setting aside money not only increases the principal for investments, but it also positively impacts the overall return, regardless of the interest rate. So, while the old cliché says one must spend money to make money, a better understanding from the examples of net-worth millionaires is that one must *save* money to make money.

Second, the pattern of net-worth millionaires debunks the myth that ordinary people do not make enough money to save. The research indicates that the individuals in the study began saving long before reaching net-worth millionaire status and have carried that habit with them through time. As Chris Hogan noted in *Everyday Millionaires*, one-third of the participants in the study never had a six-figure household income. In fact, the top three professions listed in the survey were engineer, accountant and teacher. So, these everyday millionaires did not build wealth by earning a large salary. Instead, net-worth millionaires create a plan and exercise the discipline to stick with that plan. Their ability to save up to double-digit percentages of their monthly income suggests that anyone can follow that example.

Saving in the Present. Chris Hogan and the research team discovered that everyday millionaires are not beyond hunting for bargains whenever possible. For example, ***Figure 17b*** found that more than one in three net-worth millionaires in the study said they use coupons "all the time." Another 58% use them "some of the time." Only 7% never use coupons to save money on their purchases.

Figure 17b Frequency of Millionaires' Coupon Usage

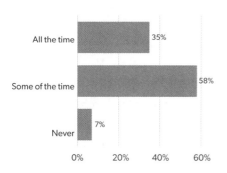

Figure 17c Millionaires Have Shopped at Thrift Stores in the Past 12 Months

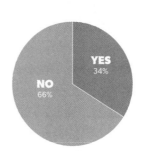

Likewise, **Figure 17c** reveals that approximately one-third of these net-worth millionaires state that they have shopped at a thrift store of some kind in the last 12 months. While the research does not indicate the kind of purchases they made, it is worth noting that so many individuals living at millionaire status have opted for secondhand clothing or other items recently.

Millionaires also used one other common tool for saving money: a shopping list. **Figure 17d** shows that many millionaires rely on a list at least some of the time when they go to the grocery store. According to the responses from the study, more than a quarter of everyday millionaires (28%) make and stick to a shopping list. Another 57% make a list and "somewhat stick to it." So, 85% of participants in the National Study of Millionaires relied on a grocery list to some degree.

Figure 17d Millionaires Using a Written Grocery List When Shopping

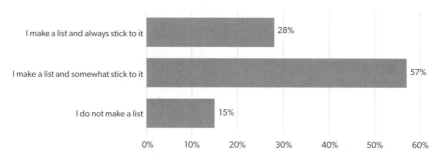

Based on the research, it seems that a substantial number of millionaires have not completely abandoned many of the frugal habits they learned early in their wealth-building journey. Even though their financial situation has expanded, they still take advantage of their old habits to continue building wealth. This is another indication that millionaires do not always act like the stereotypes so often applied to them.

MILLIONAIRES AND SPENDING

The research examined the spending habits of net-worth millionaires from several different perspectives. But three of the most interesting areas of study were shopping for groceries, eating at restaurants, and buying clothes.

GROCERIES. Based on the research, the average millionaire in this study spends approximately $412 each month on groceries as a group. Meanwhile, one report from the USDA states that a comparable family in the general population spends more than $582 a month on groceries.[4] So, in general, it can be said that net-worth millionaires are more frugal than non-millionaires in their approach to grocery shopping.

---

[4] United States Department of Agriculture, "Official USDA Food Plans: Cost of Food at Home at Four Levels, U.S. Average," March 2017.

Figure 18 breaks down how much the net-worth millionaires in the study said they spend each month on groceries. More than one-third (36%) spend less than $300 each month and almost two-thirds (64%) spend less than $450. Less than one in five (19%) spends more than $600 on groceries.

Figure 18 Millionaires' Monthly Grocery Expenditures

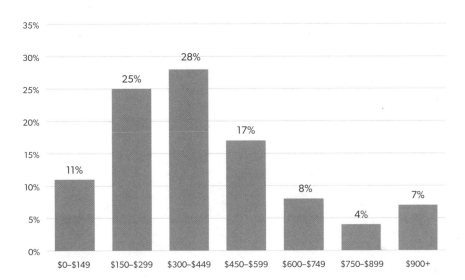

RESTAURANTS. If many net-worth millionaires limit the amount of money they spend on groceries, it is fair to wonder if they compensate by spending more at restaurants. The study results indicate that they do not. The median net-worth millionaire in this study stated that they spend less than $200 each month at restaurants. Meanwhile, the Bureau of Labor Statistics reports that the median American household spends approximately $251 eating out each month.[5]

Figure 19 demonstrates that roughly two-thirds of net-worth

[5] U.S. Bureau of Labor Statistics, "Consumer Expenditures in 2015," April 2017.

millionaires spend less than $300 at restaurants each month, with 36% spending less than $150. Only 17% spend more than $450 a month, dispelling the image of a stereotypical millionaire eating out at extravagant restaurants every night. The research shows that a vast majority of net-worth millionaires are much more frugal than their general population counterparts.

Figure 19 Millionaires' Monthly Restaurant Expenditures

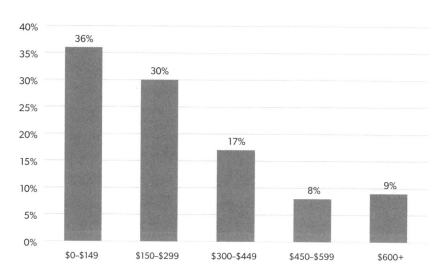

CLOTHING. Another cultural stereotype involves wealthy individuals who spend large sums of money on expensive clothes. Again, the responses provided for the National Study of Millionaires demonstrate that this stereotype is a myth. The net-worth millionaires included in this research reported that they spend an average of $117 a month on clothes, while the Bureau of Labor Statistics reports that the average American household spends $154 a month.[6]

---

[6] U.S. Bureau of Labor Statistics, "Consumer Expenditures in 2015," April 2017.

Figure 20 reveals that more than three-fourths of the net-worth millionaires in the study's random sample spend less than $150 each month on clothes. Only one in five of these individuals spend more than $200. So, as with groceries and restaurants, net-worth millionaires appear to be more frugal in their clothing budgets than members of the general population.

Figure 20 Millionaires' Monthly Clothing Expenditures

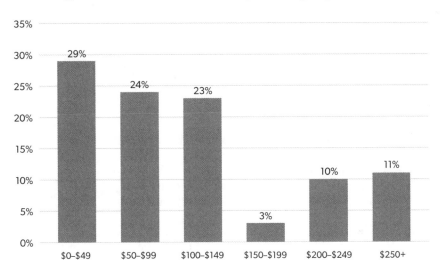

MILLIONAIRES AND CARS

To determine if net-worth millionaires display their wealth through the cars they drive, the *Everyday Millionaires* survey instrument asked participants to share information about their automobiles. The results affirmed the basic hypothesis that net-worth millionaires primarily avoid "luxury" vehicles.

Table 21 provides a percentage ranking of the automobiles driven by the net-worth millionaires in the study. The two most popular makes of cars were Toyota and Honda, with nearly one-third of all millionaires (31%) identifying one of those brands. The top American brand was Ford, placing third on the list and tying Lexus (the first luxury model mentioned) at only 8%.

While three luxury models were included in the millionaires' top 10 list, the percentages for those automobiles were relatively low. As noted, Lexus scored highest at 8%. Meanwhile, BMW and Acura accounted for only 4% and 3%, respectively. Combined, the top three luxury models garnered just 15% of the total.

These results indicate that the net-worth millionaires in this study did not necessarily favor expensive, luxury cars. As with the other categories mentioned, "frugality" is an apt descriptor of their approach to vehicles.

Table 21 Top 20 Brands of Millionaires' Cars

Car Brands of Millionaires	Market Share	Car Brands of Millionaires	Market Share
Toyota	16%	Mercedes	3%
Honda	15%	Chevrolet	3%
Ford	8%	Nissan	3%
Lexus	8%	Audi	3%
Subaru	5%	Cadillac	2%
BMW	4%	Volvo	2%
Acura	3%	Mazda	2%
Hyundai	3%	Jeep	2%
Lincoln	3%	Dodge	2%
Buick	3%	Chrysler	2%

MILLIONAIRES AND BUILDING WEALTH

Under the topic "Millionaires' Net Worth," this report considered the factors that net-worth millionaires in the study believe are important for building wealth. But this portion of the report examines the actual tools that they used to build their wealth.

The millionaires in the study were asked to share which tools they used to build their seven-figure net worth. **Table 22a** shares the percentages for the top six responses. Far and away, the millionaires view investing as the primary tool for building wealth and securing financial independence.

Eight out of 10 net-worth millionaires in the study (80%) listed investing in their employer-sponsored retirement plan as a primary vehicle for reaching that status. Meanwhile, 74% mentioned investing outside the company plan, and 73% mentioned the habit of saving money regularly.

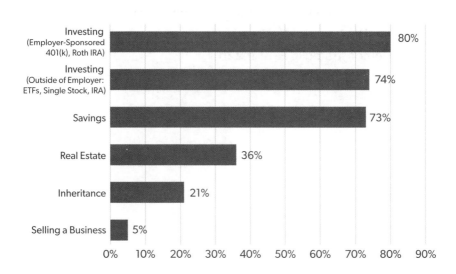

Figure 22a Percentage of Millionaires
Who Used Wealth-Building Vehicles

The importance of a company's retirement plan was not an unexpected response for the researchers. Most employer-sponsored plans are tax-favored or tax-free. They also tend to include some level of a company match that provides employees with "free" money for investing. Likewise, because most employer-sponsored plans have government-imposed annual contribution limits, it also makes sense that millionaires look for additional investing options outside of their company plan. And while the interest earned on typical savings accounts do not provide the yield of other investments, they are still reliable and safe tools for growing a margin of wealth.

After selecting which tools were used in creating financial independence, the net-worth millionaires were asked to rank each tool in order of importance. Engagement with wealth-building vehicles was critical to know, but understanding which ones had the most influence in reaching seven-figure net worth was vital. To ensure accuracy, study participants were asked which vehicles they used for building wealth and, on a later question, were shown only those items to rank by importance. This method allowed Chris Hogan and the research team to eliminate items that were not relevant to the process of building wealth and to create a set of weighted ratings for each tool. The result of those weight ratings was an "Importance Score" for each tool, as demonstrated in *Figure 22b*.

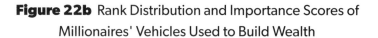

Figure 22b Rank Distribution and Importance Scores of Millionaires' Vehicles Used to Build Wealth

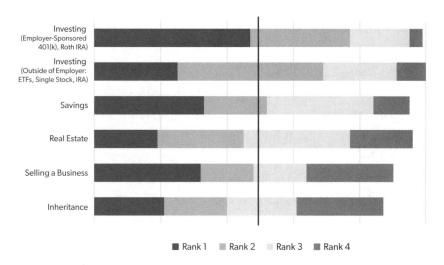

■ Rank 1　■ Rank 2　　Rank 3　■ Rank 4

Table 22c Rank Distribution and Importance Scores of Millionaires' Vehicles Used to Build Wealth

Rank Distribution	1	2	3	4	Importance Score
Investing (Employer)	47%	30%	18%	4%	6.17
Investing (Outside of Employer)	25%	44%	22%	9%	5.84
Savings	33%	19%	32%	11%	5.68
Real Estate	19%	26%	32%	19%	5.38
Selling a Business	32%	16%	16%	26%	5.32
Inheritance	21%	19%	21%	26%	5.05

For the importance score, responses were weighted so that items ranked first were given greater weight. The score, computed for each answer option/row header, is the sum of all weighted values. The weighted values were then determined by the number of columns included.

As **Table 22c** indicates, 47% of millionaires in the study ranked the employer-sponsored retirement plan first, while another 30% ranked it second. As a result, this tool ended up with the largest importance factor on the list at 6.17. When combined with information from **Figure 22a**, the research indicates that a vast majority of millionaires used a company plan to build wealth and believe it is *the primary tool* for reaching financial independence. Likewise, the millionaires also see the importance of investing outside of the company. Nearly two-thirds of respondents ranked this as either first or second, which produced a weighted importance score of 5.84. In the research interviews, millionaires mentioned taking advantage of IRAs and ETFs (specifically low-cost index funds) as some of the keys to growing their wealth.

Two tools that do not appear to be high priorities for the net-worth millionaires are selling a business and receiving an inheritance. Less than half of millionaires who sold businesses (48%) ranked this in the top two on their lists and earned an importance score of only 5.32. This was somewhat surprising, because one might assume that the sale of the company would produce a sizable windfall. This may be related to the types of businesses being sold—small businesses, such as landscaping companies or home appraisal services. It's unlikely the sale netted millions in profit—perhaps a few hundred thousand—thereby leading the owner to rely on additional avenues of building wealth.

Likewise, inheritances ranked at the bottom of the millionaires' list with an importance score of 5.05. Only one in five net-worth millionaires who received an inheritance placed it first in their rankings.

The next section of the research provides some explanation as to why the net-worth millionaires in this study downplayed the role of inheritances in their efforts to build wealth.

MILLIONAIRES AND INHERITANCES

As noted above, the research identified a discrepancy between how the net-worth millionaires viewed the role of inheritances in building wealth and how the general population perceived inheritances. In general, the millionaires downplayed the importance of inheritances, while non-millionaires considered them second only to financial discipline in a list of factors that contribute to millionaire status. In addition, only 4% of millionaires in the study ranked it first in terms of tools used for building wealth, producing the lowest importance score at 5.05.

A deeper dive into the research demonstrates that the net-worth millionaires' own experiences could explain why they see inheritances differently than the general population. *Figure 23* reveals that 79% of all millionaires in the study have never received an inheritance. It should be noted that 21% did receive an inheritance, which roughly aligns with what government data from the U.S. Bureau of Labor Statistics has found in the general population.[7] Millionaires are no more likely to receive an inheritance than the average American.

It is safe to say very few of these individuals relied on inherited money to build their financial independence. Of those who received an inheritance, few received a large enough inheritance to actually move the needle in their financial lives. Approximately half of these individuals were given less than $250,000. While this would certainly help in one's journey toward a seven-figure net worth, it typically is not enough to push a portfolio over the top. Other investments and savings are necessary for an individual to become a net-worth millionaire.

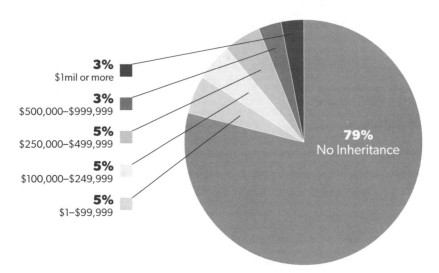

Figure 23 Millionaires and Inheritances Received

3%
$1mil or more

3%
$500,000–$999,999

5%
$250,000–$499,999

5%
$100,000–$249,999

5%
$1–$99,999

79%
No Inheritance

Even adding the next level of the pie chart into the equation does not significantly change the impact of inheritances on an individual's ability to reach millionaire status. As stated, approximately one in nine millionaires received less than $250,000. Adding the next sliver indicates that 94% of all millionaires in the study received less than $500,000. Again, this is undeniably a large number, but it is not the sole factor in these individuals becoming net-worth millionaires.

According to this research, only 3% of the respondents received an inheritance of at least $1 million—essentially securing net-worth millionaire status. The vast majority of them built wealth through other tools, such as employer-sponsored retirement plans and other investments outside of a company plan.

CONCLUSION

The Ramsey Solutions research team set out to conduct the largest study of net-worth millionaires ever. Between the qualitative and quantitative phases of the research, this effort included the responses of more than 10,000 net-worth millionaires, including a statistically significant random sample of 2,000 millionaires with no prior connection to Ramsey Solutions. It also provided comparison criteria through a random general population sampling of 2,000 individuals.

As stated in this paper's introduction, the purpose of the study was to determine the validity of the following alternative hypothesis: *Millionaires gain wealth through specific choices, such as working hard, demonstrating financial discipline, and investing consistently and wisely over time.* This working hypothesis would not only identify key characteristics that individuals can use in finding financial independence, but it would also debunk several myths and misunderstandings about building wealth that might be common in the general population.

After analyzing the results of this extensive study, Chris Hogan and the research team can assert with a degree of confidence that the alternative hypothesis was validated. Over and over and in multiple ways, millionaires stated a reliance on elements within their control—such as positive work ethic, self-determination and personal responsibility—rather than elements they could not control—such as luck, socioeconomic upbringing or large inheritances—to gain their net-worth millionaire status and their financial independence.

Among the insights gained from the research:

- Net-worth millionaires generally steer clear of debt in any form. For example, almost three-quarters of millionaires in the study had never had either credit card debt (73%) or student loan debt (71%). More than nine in 10 have never even paid a utility bill late.

- Net-worth millionaires tend to demonstrate a "growth mindset" rather than a "fixed mindset"—a mentality of abundance rather than scarcity. They embrace change and usually see adversity as an opportunity for growth. Perseverance is a key quality for net-worth millionaires.
- Net-worth millionaires tend to be frugal—not flashy. Instead of diving into extravagance, the millionaires in the study spend less than the general population on groceries, restaurants and clothing. Most also drive moderately priced cars and live in houses that are smaller than the national average. More than half live in neighborhoods where the average household income is less than $75,000 a year.
- Net-worth millionaires consider financial discipline and consistent investing as the primary tools for building financial independence. The most important priorities for the millionaires in this study include the following: taking advantage of employer-provided retirement plans, investing outside of company plans, and saving in other areas.
- Net-worth millionaires generally downplay the importance of luck and inheritances. Since they emphasize things they can control, they do not believe luck has had an impact on their financial success. And because only one in five millionaires in the study has received an inheritance, it does not represent a reliable tool in building wealth.
- Net-worth millionaires believe that virtually anyone can follow their path and become a millionaire. The millionaires in the study do not believe wealth building is a quick or easy process. It has taken most of them decades to reach a seven-figure net worth. But they demonstrate a confidence that

anyone can reach this milestone through discipline and hard work over time.

The depth of this research has yielded a vast quantity of reliable information and insights related to the mindset and behaviors of "everyday" millionaires that could open doors for additional research in this field in the years to come. While this white paper includes deeper dives into several areas of the National Study of Millionaires research, even more information is included in the attached appendix. This could provide interested parties with even more data for comparison and further study.

However, it should be emphasized that this paper—along with the research upon which it is based—is not designed solely to outline academic theory. Like Chris Hogan's book *Everyday Millionaires*, it contains practical suggestions for individuals who might strive to reach net-worth millionaire status. It holds the key to creating financial independence, which can make a difference for countless families and their communities.

APPENDIX

The following section of the report contains tables and cross tabulations on various topics from the National Study of Millionaires. The raw data allows one to study the numbers and draw conclusions not included in the white paper.

APPENDIX A
The Mean Age at Which
Millionaire Status Was Achieved, by Cohort

Millionaire Status Achieved	Average Age
Overall Age	50
By Birth Order	
First	50
Middle	51
Youngest	48
Only	47
By Type of Student	
A Student	49
B Student	51
C Student	50
By Type of College	
Public	50
Private	49
Ivy League	48
Community	52
By Education Level	
No degree	53
Bachelor's	50
Graduate	48
Terminal	50
By Upbringing	
Lower Class	50
Lower-Middle Class	51
Middle Class	51

The Mean Age at Which
Millionaire Status Was Achieved, by Cohort

Upper-Middle Class	46
Upper Class	36
By Books Read Per Year	
0	50
1–5	50
6–10	50
11 or More	48
By Budget Frequency	
Rarely/Never	50
Some Months	48
Most Months	47

APPENDIX B

*The Median and Average Net Worth
of Study Participants, by Cohort*

Net Worth	Median	Average
Overall Net Worth	$2,485,000	$3,544,535
By Region		
Northeast	$2,677,400	$3,774,181
Midwest	$2,202,500	$3,093,377
South	$2,340,000	$3,499,407
West	$2,500,000	$3,745,194
By Area		
Urban	$2,750,000	$4,051,116
Suburban	$2,500,000	$3,492,133
Rural	$2,057,500	$3,188,598
By Birth Order		
First	$2,500,000	$3,694,564
Middle	$2,100,000	$2,974,581
Youngest	$2,500,000	$3,625,068
Only	$2,817,500	$3,864,104
By Type of Student		
A Student	$2,500,000	$3,716,774
B Student	$2,397,000	$3,014,225
C Student	$2,500,000	$4,509,344
By Type of College		
Public	$2,340,000	$3,430,463
Private	$2,494,000	$3,847,615
Ivy League	$3,330,000	$5,096,412
Community	$2,000,000	$2,694,575
By Education Level		
No degree	$2,600,000	$3,047,317

APPENDIX B *(continued)*
The Median and Average Net Worth
of Study Participants, by Cohort

Net Worth	Median	Average
Bachelor's	$2,250,000	$3,135,537
Graduate	$2,465,000	$3,519,799
Terminal	$3,400,000	$5,353,543
By Upbringing		
Lower Class	$2,440,000	$2,965,184
Lower-Middle Class	$2,485,000	$3,149,763
Middle Class	$2,300,000	$3,538,370
Upper-Middle Class	$2,625,000	$3,765,220
Upper Class	$6,000,000	$13,202,222
Overall Net Worth	$2,485,000	$3,544,535
By By Books Read Per Year		
0	$2,350,000	$3,785,843
1–5	$2,380,000	$3,388,329
6–10	$2,500,000	$3,229,825
11 or More	$2,500,000	$3,953,158
By Personality		
Introvert	$2,300,000	$3,396,074
Extrovert	$2,500,000	$3,718,052
By Relationship Status		
Married	$2,500,000	$3,539,520
Single	$2,300,000	$3,218,905
Divorced	$2,375,000	$3,033,821
By Career Satisfaction		
Love my work	$2,500,000	$3,800,549
Neutral about my work	$2,163,000	$3,193,973
I do not like my work	$1,900,000	$2,400,568s

APPENDIX C

Ownership of Primary Residence, Estimated Home Value and Square Footage, by Cohort

Primary Residence	Paid-For Residence	Median Home Value	Average Value	Median Square Footage	Average Square Footage
Overall	68%	$450,000	$631,364	2,500	2,638
By Region					
Northeast	74%	$500,000	$680,995	2,500	2,607
Midwest	69%	$325,000	$403,046	2,500	2,741
South	68%	$412,500	$530,647	2,600	2,793
West	63%	$650,000	$892,438	2,300	2,422
By Area					
Urban	67%	$550,000	$753,519	2,000	2,266
Suburban	67%	$450,000	$632,832	2,500	2,746
Rural	75%	$385,000	$493,487	2,400	2,621
By Household Size					
1	72%	$375,000	$590,959	1,990	2,081
2	73%	$450,000	$596,052	2,500	2,627
3	62%	$550,000	$902,034	3,000	2,943
4	39%	$455,000	$653,346	2,800	3,040
5 or More	48%	$520,000	$588,864	2,950	3,235
By Net Worth					
$1mil–$1.99mil	56%	$375,000	$446,681	2,300	2,378
$2mil–$2.99mil	76%	$400,000	$498,500	2,400	2,562
$3mil–$3.99mil	74%	$500,000	$616,374	2,500	2,646
$4mil–$4.99mil	76%	$650,000	$781,657	2,500	2,789
$5mil+	76%	$750,000	$1,137,933	3,200	3,360

Ownership of Primary Residence, Estimated Home Value and Square Footage, by Cohort

By Age					
Under 45	36%	$540,000	$685,930	2,450	2,711
45–54	49%	$450,000	$810,622	2,500	2,790
55–64	65%	$410,000	$545,648	2,500	2,623
65–74	75%	$450,000	$566,470	2,500	2,654
75 or Older	92%	$482,500	$639,035	2,300	2,466
By Upbringing					
Lower Class	68%	$492,500	$540,250	2,600	2,772
Lower-Middle Class	73%	$425,000	$553,938	2,400	2,552
Middle Class	69%	$425,000	$625,925	2,400	2,575
Upper-Middle Class	60%	$537,500	$763,651	2,800	2,840
Upper Class	57%	$600,000	$974,333	3,600	3,444

APPENDIX D

Type of Primary Residence, by Cohort
(not all cohorts add to 100 due to senior-living facilities,
living with family, etc.)

Type of Primary Residence	House	Town House/ Condo	Apartment
Overall	82%	13%	4%
By Region			
Northeast	76%	14%	8%
Midwest	88%	10%	2%
South	81%	15%	3%
West	84%	11%	4%
By Area			
Urban	62%	24%	13%
Suburban	86%	11%	2%
Rural	91%	5%	2%
By Household Size			
1	57%	29%	14%
2	84%	12%	3%
3	94%	4%	2%
4	97%	0%	1%
5 or More	100%	0%	0%
By Net Worth			
$1mil–$1.99mil	82%	13%	4%
$2mil–$2.99mil	81%	13%	5%
$3mil–$3.99mil	85%	11%	2%
$4mil–$4.99mil	85%	11%	5%
$5mil+	75%	16%	7%

APPENDIX D *(continued)*
Type of Primary Residence, by Cohort
(not all cohorts add to 100 due to senior-living facilities, living with family, etc.)

By Age			
Under 45	76%	11%	11%
45–54	87%	7%	5%
55–64	85%	12%	2%
65–74	81%	14%	4%
75 or Older	74%	11%	5%
By Upbringing			
Lower Class	86%	7%	5%
Lower-Middle Class	84%	11%	3%
Middle Class	82%	13%	5%
Upper-Middle Class	76%	17%	6%
Upper Class	86%	9%	5%

APPENDIX E

Years to Pay Off Primary Residence, by Cohort

Years To Pay Off Primary Residence	Average
Overall	10.2 years
By Region	
Northeast	10.9
Midwest	10.4
South	8.4
West	11.7
By Area	
Urban	10.1
Suburban	11.3
Rural	6.9
By Net Worth	
$1mil–$1.99mil	12
$2mil–$2.99mil	9.7
$3mil–$3.99mil	10.3
$4mil–$4.99mil	9.1
$5mil+	7.9
By Years to Become Millionaire	
10 or Less	5.9
11–20	7.2
21–30	10.0
31–40	12.1
40+	12.7

APPENDIX E *(continued)*
Years to Pay Off Primary Residence, by Cohort

By Upbringing	
Lower Class	9.6
Lower-Middle Class	10.7
Middle Class	10.2
Upper-Middle Class	10.1
Upper Class	8.9

APPENDIX F
Monthly Grocery Expenditure, by Cohort

Monthly Grocery Expenditure	Average
Overall Expenditure	$412
By Region	
Northeast	$414
Midwest	$405
South	$401
West	$429
By Area	
Urban	$392
Suburban	$416
Rural	$408
By Household Size	
1	$231
2	$408
3	$513
4	$538
5 or More	$561
By Net Worth	
$1mil–$1.99mil	$417
$2mil–$2.99mil	$390
$3mil–$3.99mil	$361
$4mil–$4.99mil	$388
$5mil+	$505
By Employment Status	
Working	$424
Retired	$373

APPENDIX F *(continued)*
Monthly Grocery Expenditure, by Cohort

By Age	
Under 45	$421
45–54	$487
55–64	$426
65–74	$379
75 or Older	$364

APPENDIX G
Monthly Restaurant Expenditure, by Cohort

Monthly Restaurant Expenditure	Average
Overall Expenditure	$267
By Region	
Northeast	$292
Midwest	$279
South	$256
West	$250
By Area	
Urban	$290
Suburban	$277
Rural	$179
By Household Size	
1	$185
2	$278
3	$246
4	$322
5 or More	$296
By Budget Frequency	
Rarely/Never	$270
Some Months	$292
Most Months	$214

APPENDIX G *(continued)*
Monthly Restaurant Expenditure, by Cohort

By Net Worth	
$1mil–$1.99mil	$250
$2mil–$2.99mil	$226
$3mil–$3.99mil	$310
$4mil–$4.99mil	$262
$5mil+	$320
By Employment Status	
Working	$282
Retired	$245
By Coupon Usage	
Use Coupons	$222
Don't Use Coupons	$345
By Personality	
Introvert	$234
Extrovert	$304

APPENDIX H

Monthly Clothing Expenditure, by Cohort

Monthly Clothing Expenditure	Average Expenditure
Overall Expenditure	$117
By Region	
Northeast	$114
Midwest	$133
South	$115
West	$113
By Area	
Urban	$134
Suburban	$123
Rural	$70
By Household Size	
1	$108
2	$103
3	$135
4	$178
5 or More	$186
By Net Worth	
$1mil–$1.99mil	$100
$2mil–$2.99mil	$95
$3mil–$3.99mil	$112
$4mil–$4.99mil	$123
$5mil+	$165

APPENDIX H *(continued)*
Monthly Clothing Expenditure, by Cohort

By Employment Status	
Working	$136
Retired	$84
By Age	
Under 45	$244
45–54	$151
55–64	$118
65–74	$94
75 or Older	$82

APPENDIX I

Vehicles Used to Build Wealth, by Cohort

Building Wealth	Investing (Company)	Investing (Individual)	Real Estate	Inheritance	Selling a Business	Income to Savings (More Than 15%)	Used Financial Planner
Overall	80%	74%	36%	21%	5%	48%	68%
By Region							
Northeast	78%	74%	33%	22%	5%	45%	67%
Midwest	83%	75%	27%	20%	5%	52%	71%
South	82%	75%	36%	20%	4%	49%	65%
West	75%	73%	44%	20%	6%	44%	70%
By Area							
Urban	74%	75%	40%	23%	3%	49%	67%
Suburban	81%	73%	34%	19%	5%	47%	69%
Rural	84%	78%	34%	23%	6%	47%	69%
By Age							
Under 45	70%	62%	41%	8%	3%	54%	59%
45–54	76%	73%	32%	14%	3%	59%	63%
55–64	84%	71%	30%	16%	6%	57%	65%
65–74	84%	79%	41%	25%	4%	41%	71%
75 or Older	75%	77%	38%	30%	7%	32%	75%
By Net Worth							
$1mil–$1.99mil	84%	74%	34%	22%	5%	43%	69%
$2mil–$2.99mil	84%	81%	31%	18%	2%	48%	67%
$3mil–$3.99mil	82%	78%	39%	20%	6%	46%	69%
$4mil–$4.99mil	80%	82%	39%	25%	5%	57%	67%
$5mil+	72%	71%	48%	25%	9%	55%	66%
By Upbringing							
Lower Class	79%	81%	42%	14%	2%	58%	67%
Lower-Middle Class	82%	78%	35%	19%	5%	45%	65%

APPENDIX I *(continued)*
Vehicles Used to Build Wealth, by Cohort

Middle Class	82%	75%	36%	21%	5%	49%	69%
Upper-Middle Class	72%	67%	34%	25%	5%	45%	69%
Upper Class	64%	55%	45%	14%	0%	41%	91%
Overall	80%	74%	36%	21%	5%	48%	68%
By Education Level							
No degree	67%	74%	36%	14%	8%	52%	64%
Bachelor's	78%	73%	35%	21%	5%	46%	70%
Graduate	82%	76%	32%	21%	4%	47%	68%
Terminal	82%	74%	40%	24%	3%	49%	72%
By Type of College							
Public	82%	74%	35%	21%	4%	49%	67%
Private	81%	76%	34%	21%	4%	48%	70%
Ivy League	81%	77%	44%	28%	3%	33%	71%
Community	87%	79%	39%	23%	9%	57%	72%
By Books Read Per Year							
0	80%	71%	34%	15%	4%	57%	59%
1–5	77%	72%	36%	21%	5%	44%	72%
6–10	83%	77%	34%	22%	6%	40%	69%
11 or More	83%	81%	37%	23%	4%	52%	70%
By Years to Become Millionaire							
10 or Less	55%	68%	55%	18%	5%	48%	50%
11–20	80%	77%	34%	11%	5%	64%	63%
21–30	82%	79%	37%	14%	4%	53%	62%
31–40	84%	73%	33%	29%	4%	39%	74%
40+	81%	77%	36%	42%	2%	33%	77%

APPENDIX J
Common Beliefs in General Population, by Cohort

General Population	Belief 1	Belief 2	Belief 3	Belief 4	Belief 5
Overall	86%	77%	67%	62%	62%
By Region					
Northeast	82%	81%	74%	65%	67%
Midwest	87%	79%	63%	63%	58%
South	84%	69%	66%	60%	59%
West	87%	80%	73%	69%	64%
By Area					
Urban	85%	76%	69%	64%	62%
Rural	90%	81%	60%	56%	62%
By Generation					
Baby Boomer	85%	70%	59%	52%	53%
Generation X	89%	78%	72%	69%	68%
Millennials	82%	86%	77%	74%	69%
By Education Level					
No Degree	93%	86%	58%	59%	47%
Bachelor's	85%	74%	64%	55%	57%
Graduate	86%	77%	64%	58%	59%
Terminal	85%	76%	73%	71%	71%

BELIEF 1
Wealthy people use debt in their favor to make more money.

BELIEF 2
Most wealthy people come from wealthy families.

BELIEF 3
To become rich, you have to take big risks with your money.

APPENDIX J *(continued)*
Common Beliefs in General Population, by Cohort

By Upbringing					
Lower Class	84%	74%	77%	66%	67%
Lower-Middle Class	87%	77%	69%	63%	64%
Middle Class	86%	78%	68%	62%	60%
Upper-Middle Class	86%	77%	58%	62%	60%
Upper Class	74%	71%	67%	76%	56%
By Type of College					
Public	89%	78%	67%	60%	59%
Private	82%	76%	61%	59%	56%
Ivy League	92%	83%	60%	56%	54%
Community	83%	80%	70%	70%	61%
By Outlook					
Optimist	87%	75%	69%	62%	60%
Pessimist	81%	84%	63%	66%	66%

BELIEF 4
The majority of millionaires inherited their money.

BELIEF 5
You need a six-figure salary to become a millionaire in today's economy.

APPENDIX J *(continued)*
Common Beliefs in General Population, by Cohort

General Population	Belief 6	Belief 7	Belief 8	Belief 9	Belief 10
Overall	56%	51%	45%	25%	18%
By Region					
Northeast	63%	60%	53%	26%	21%
Midwest	53%	50%	43%	21%	15%
South	51%	45%	42%	25%	17%
West	61%	53%	45%	30%	18%
By Area					
Urban	57%	52%	45%	26%	18%
Rural	53%	48%	46%	19%	17%
By Generation					
Baby Boomer	43%	45%	38%	18%	10%
Generation X	64%	52%	50%	27%	23%
Millennials	67%	60%	52%	31%	26%
By Education Level					
No Degree	40%	58%	44%	29%	18%
Bachelor's	50%	44%	37%	18%	13%
Graduate	52%	50%	41%	27%	20%
Terminal	66%	55%	54%	26%	20%

BELIEF 6
Most millionaires have a million-dollar home.

BELIEF 7
You have to be lucky to get rich.

BELIEF 8
Wealthy people are materialistic, self-centered, and obsessed with having more.

By Upbringing					
Lower Class	58%	57%	59%	20%	24%
Lower-Middle Class	57%	50%	44%	20%	14%
Middle Class	57%	50%	44%	26%	18%
Upper-Middle Class	48%	52%	41%	27%	16%
Upper Class	63%	68%	50%	60%	53%
By Type of College					
Public	54%	52%	41%	27%	16%
Private	44%	48%	38%	17%	14%
Ivy League	64%	67%	45%	33%	33%
Community	56%	43%	41%	20%	17%
By Outlook					
Optimist	56%	48%	43%	25%	17%
Pessimist	57%	58%	50%	24%	21%

BELIEF 9
To become rich, you need to act rich.

BELIEF 10
If you're born into a poor family, you can't become wealthy.

APPENDIX K

Becoming a Millionaire Is More About Personal Habits or External Circumstances, by Cohort

Becoming a Millionaire Is More About . . .	Personal Habits	External Circumstances
Overall	84%	16%
By Region		
Northeast	81%	19%
Midwest	87%	13%
South	84%	16%
West	86%	14%
By Area		
Urban	77%	23%
Suburban	87%	13%
Rural	86%	14%
By Upbringing		
Lower Class	84%	16%
Lower-Middle Class	87%	13%
Middle Class	85%	15%
Upper-Middle Class	79%	21%
Upper Class	83%	17%
By Net Worth		
$1mil–$1.99mil	87%	13%
$2mil–$2.99mil	85%	15%
$3mil–$3.99mil	80%	20%
$4mil–$4.99mil	83%	17%
$5mil+	87%	13%

APPENDIX K *(continued)*
Becoming a Millionaire Is More About Personal Habits or External Circumstances, by Cohort

By Years to Become Millionaire		
10 or Less	76%	24%
11–20	86%	14%
21–30	88%	12%
31–40	84%	16%
40+	80%	20%
By Birth Order		
First	82%	18%
Middle	88%	12%
Youngest	88%	12%
Only	79%	21%
Overall	84%	16%
By Type of Student		
A Student	82%	18%
B Student	88%	12%
C Student	88%	12%
By Type of College		
Public	84%	16%
Private	83%	17%
Ivy League	80%	20%
Community	88%	12%

Becoming a Millionaire Is More About Personal Habits or External Circumstances, by Cohort

By Education Level			
No Degree	89%	11%	
Bachelor's	88%	12%	
Graduate	83%	17%	
Terminal	74%	26%	
By Books Read Per Year			
0	87%	13%	
1–5	84%	16%	
6–10	85%	15%	
11 or More	81%	19%	
By Age			
Under 45	75%	25%	
45–54	85%	15%	
55–64	86%	14%	
65–74	87%	13%	
75 or Older	82%	18%	
By Sleep Pattern			
Early Riser	86%	14%	
Night Owl	80%	20%	
By Outlook			
Optimist	87%	13%	
Pessimist	72%	28%	

CHECK OUT CHRIS HOGAN'S #1 NATIONAL BEST-SELLING BOOK

EVERYDAY MILLIONAIRES

CHRISHOGAN360.COM